This book
Right of Passage
*concerns youth service
and focuses on
a human, not a political, agenda.*
– N.G.C.

RIGHT OF PASSAGE

The Heroic Journey to Adulthood

Nancy Geyer Christopher

Cornell Press
Washington, D.C.

Printed in the United States of America

1 3 5 7 9 10 8 6 4 2

ISBN 0-9652719-2-7

Library of Congress Catalog Card Number: 96-85099

1. Cultural Studies—United States. 2. Adolescence—United States. 3. Youth Service—United States

Includes resource directory, self-evaluation, notes and index.

How to Order: Ask for this book at your local bookstore. Or, with major credit card, you may order toll-free via 1-800-879-4214. Price $15 plus shipping and handling. Quantity discounts are available, especially to non-profit organizations for their fund-raising projects and youth development programs.

Cornell Press
P.O. Box 25798
Washington, DC 20007-8798
Publisher of books to enhance our quality of life.
SAN 299-0245

Prayer for Our Youth
Psalm 144: 11-12

. . . Deliver me from the hand of
strange children,
whose mouth speaketh vanity,
and their right hand is a right hand
of falsehood:

[Release us from false perceptions.]

That our sons may be as plants
grown up in their youth;
that our daughters may be as
cornerstones, polished after
the similitude of a palace:

*[Help us to see the potential
of our young people
that our vision may free them
to discover their true identity.]*

CONTENTS

* * *

Acknowledgments

We seldom realize it, but sharing a story from our life with another is an act of great trust. For that reason I must acknowledge the generosity of more than four dozen people who were willing to share their stories with me. Their identity is disguised to protect their privacy. The telling of their stories took many hundreds of hours over the past seven years.

My husband, Lawrence Cornell Christopher, was with me during a number of these lengthy interviews, drawing on his own background in journalism and broadcasting, to raise questions of which I had not thought. In addition, he engaged with me in thousands of hours of discussion as I searched for the internal logic of these stories to weave them together. We would go back time and again to our own life stories to become aware of the pitfalls and roadblocks that we too faced in trying to grow up. We would remember, with gratitude, the support and inspiration we found along the way. He made it possible for me to leave full-time teaching in order to work on this compelling project. Furthermore, he never once said, "Stop! I don't want to hear any more," when I would bring up a point for the umpteenth time, but would listen to me with patience and engage in yet another discussion.

My adult children, Kateri Geyer Young and Peter Geyer, were also patient with their Mom for grilling them on their passages from adolescence to adulthood, and they even read portions of the manuscript and offered comments.

In addition, I am enormously grateful to Donald Eberly, founder in 1966 and former director of the National Service Secretariat, for his interest and his openness to hours of discussion, for his advice and moral support, and—through his books and articles—for expanding my view of the power of service.

So too, Alec and Mora Dickson, founders in 1958 of the British Overseas Volunteer Corps (British Peace Corps) and Community Volunteer Service (the domestic counterpart), who inspired me with their life-long commitment to the value of youth service, both to the server and to the served. Elisabeth Hoodliss, present director of the CVS, whom we interviewed in London, warned me not to forget the importance of those served in emphasizing the value to the server.

Early in my project Patricia Flederman, from Cape Town, South Africa, gave me insight into the service program in Botswana, based on her research there. She returned later to the United States in time to read my manuscript at a critical point and to make suggestions.

During the early writing stage Denise Doolan, a Washington, D.C., artist and a master of metaphor, spent hours discussing with me various ways of looking at rites of passage. Ed Kemp, a member of the U.S. Department of State and a former journalist, also gave critical advice regarding format and content. My developing understanding of ritual and rites of passage owes much to Dr. Lee Roloff of Northwestern University Department of Performance Studies. My years of work with high school students were enhanced by the compassionate guidance of educator William Freisem. Early discussions with Sharon Dole and Geri French, both mothers of recent teenagers and both involved in education in the Chicago area, helped me refine my ideas about steering teenagers through the shoals of adolescence.

During the process of writing this book, Louise Carus Mahdi invited me to collaborate with her as co-editor of anthology, *Crossroads: The Quest for Contemporary Rites of Passage* (1996) for Open Court Publishing Company. The hours we spent together deliberating, discussing, and debating rites of passage enriched both of us. Louise's assistant, Susan Rublaitus, with her superb organizational and editing skills, kept both of us focused on the task.

My writing peers at the Bethesda Writer's Center were enormously helpful in shaking me out of academic jargon in the early drafts. My friend Win Finegan, who was co-editor with me of our high school newspaper, warned me in an early draft, "Let's cut to the story." Jane Partridge, with her three decades in secondary education, was very helpful in reading and commenting on the manuscript, not only as a teacher and parent, but as an expert in English and the humanities. Katharine Forsyth BVM, also a Chicago educator, read the manuscript and made comments from the perspective of higher education as did Linda Chisholm, who viewed the heroic journey in the context of international education.

At another critical stage my sister-in-law, Cathy Jorgensen Itnyre, a professor of history and philosophy in Southern California, brought her keen sense of logic to the manuscript and offered clarifying suggestions. My sister Brigid Kelly, a ballet dancer and teacher, not only spent hours late at night poring over the manuscript, but called my attention to "confirmation" as a social act as well as a religious ritual. Without realizing it, she was "confirming" her sister as an author. And finally, I give thanks to my parents, Robert and Dolores Itnyre, who somehow survived my own stormy adolescence and who helped me to realize we are never through with trying to grow up.

New York book veteran Michael Monbeck helped prepare the manuscript for printing. I am thankful for his technical help.

For these and all the other acts of gracious giving—of time, of advice, of stories—I am extraordinarily grateful. Any shortcomings in the book are my own responsibility.

* * *

Crossing Bridges

As an adolescent I lived in a small city embracing two sides of a river with the business district on an island in the middle.

To move around the city at all demanded frequent crossing of bridges. Nightly I would walk to a bridge—not always the same one—to make my way across.

Some nights the bridge I chose would lead down into the dark murky water below. Other nights on another bridge I could see big gaps between its wooden planks. By day these same bridges were reasonably solid. I crossed them with little concern for my safety. By night they became death-traps to which my feet, at someone's bidding other than my own, invariably led me.

Night after night I was drawn to the bridges, facing the terror of crossing, yet knowing I must get to the other side. Then, at the touch of the dark water, I would awake in panic.

Three decades later and far from that small city of many bridges, I am tutoring a 35-year-old man in an adult literacy program. The tutoring is taking place at a large urban library. He tells me about entering high school, after absences and other delays, at the age of 17:

> This was the first time I was exposed to literature. It was in ninth grade. I wasn't doing that well in most of my subjects. But I read this book about Achilles. It was just so, so hero-ish. It was so epic and adventurous. To that degree, I myself . . . I was Achilles when I read this book. I can remember reading this and just getting pumped up and influenced. I can remember—I was living at the [juvenile] home then—I came down the steps, and one of the kids I was living with came bounding down the steps after me. And I was already out the door and ready for school because always in the back of my mind was the *Iliad* with all this adventure. So when I came down the steps, he could see it immediately, and he said in a contemptive sort of disgust, "Yeah, who are ya today?" To me—I thought to myself—I am Achilles.

Each of us was trying to live out our adolescent heroic journey, I by crossing treacherous bridges, he by going out to fight his daily battles as Achilles. Neither of us had a clue about the psychological drama playing itself out in our imagination, and we had no idea at the time that we were answering some kind of inner call.

My attempts to grow up caused family crises. As a senior in high school I announced I was going to become a Maryknoll nun. My parents, unnerved by the news, begged me to wait. All right, I was willing to hold off awhile. But several years later in college, when I announced that I planned to marry my current boyfriend, another crisis erupted. My father wouldn't hear of my leaving school; my mother had a fit that I would even consider marriage as a teenager.

If I had been ready to grow up, I would have gone ahead and become a nun—or a bride. But I couldn't bear to hurt my parents. And I dreaded crossing the bridge alone. It was time to grow up, but I didn't know how.

As a compromise with my parents, I left full-time school and worked part-time in a local hospital. It was a relief to get out of the classroom and into "real life" where I could see my small tasks—giving back rubs, feeding the sick, and cheering the depressed—have some effect and where my co-workers treated me as an adult. The recurring nightmares eventually stopped.

Later, I went back to college with a sense of being connected to a bigger world out there. I avoided a premature marriage and, if I had grown up somewhat in the process, it was more because of my perception of contributing something worthwhile to the world than because of what I was learning in class. If only the classroom had amplified what I was doing in the real world, but that was an idea whose time was yet to come. Meanwhile, I still didn't understand what was happening to me, and I continued to stumble around for the next couple of decades, not certain of what would *really* mark my arrival into adulthood.

My literacy friend, so full of his Achilles-spirit at age 17, so brimming with hope and energy, and so anxious to begin his own heroic journey, quit school in the ninth grade to seek his destiny. He got out of the classroom into "real life" real fast and at the same time lost contact with any kind of guiding wisdom to ensure he would learn essential life skills. Now, eighteen years and many jobs later, he feels like a horse trapped behind the starting gate. His poetic spirit rouses itself periodically from his addiction to crack cocaine and he tries once more to take control of his life.

For both of us, our worlds at a certain point in adolescence had grown too small. We followed an irresistible urge to expand our horizons and, in the process, kind of bumbled our ways into adulthood. I was fortunate to have the safety net of a caring—though fearful—family and the opportunity to try myself out in adult activity that was personally satisfying. My friend had no intact family and no adult-guided opportunities.

Neither of us was conscious of the ancient pattern of the heroic journey into adulthood to which we were responding. Had we known, we might have saved ourselves much agony and many dead ends. And even more important, if the adults in our lives had been aware . . . If the adults in the lives of *all* teenagers were aware of the heroic journey pattern and its implications for healthy development, they might be more helpful in guiding their young in this critical passage.

I have realized in the intervening decades that adolescents must *earn* their right to adulthood and adults must *support* that right. Looking at tribal and traditional rites of passage can give us clues to ways today's teenagers might earn their right as well as the role the adult community must play.

This is a book about an ancient pattern that repeats itself in each generation. It is about a vocabulary for describing that pattern and how it works itself out in the complicated journey to maturity. And finally is it about how American culture has been—and might continue to be—supportive of healthy and challenging ways for our young to *earn their right of passage* into adulthood.

* * *

Part I. Rite of Passage

Metaphors for Growing Up

> ***metaphor*** (met'a for) n. From Greek, Latin, Old French;
> to carry or transfer name or description
> of one thing or object to another, often by
> implication or analogy. 1. figure of speech
> 2. allegory 3. parable 4. story.

M etaphors are a cultural "lens." A kind of ministory, they filter our view of the world. Someone who looks at his life as "a bowl full of cherries" will have quite a different take on it than someone else who thinks her life is "the pits." Metaphors shape public as well as personal imagination and frame our expectations. No one can deny, for example, the power of "the American dream."

But consider looking at, or framing, the process of coming to adulthood with a metaphor like "rite of passage." You might well respond, "It depends on *what* is considered a rite of passage."

Ah, *that* is the sticking point.

That sticking point is the subject of Chapter One, which examines the media use and often abuse of "rite of passage." In addition, Chapter One compares the contemporary image with the traditional meaning of the term. Chapter Two explores what religious ritual has to tell us about coming to maturity. Chapter Three discusses clues to maturity from the perspective of developmental psychology.

Chapter One

Rite of Passage:
Here's the Concept but Where's the
Reality?

What happens when a metaphor like "rite of passage" is seized by the media and imprinted relentlessly on the public consciousness? Especially if it refers to destructive or trivial behavior? Think about the following activities: smoking that first cigarette, getting drunk during freshman year in college (or worst, freshman year in high school), going overseas as part of a military operation, passing the driver's test and getting a license, starting a first job, graduating from high school or college, going to jail and returning to the peer-community a hero.

Each of these experiences is very different. Yet all are described as a "rite of passage," as though the term should trigger in the reader an insight that will tie together such diverse activities. The increasing use of the term in the media over the past two decades has raised its profile but diffused its meaning. My curiosity led me to conduct a mass media survey. I found only one reference in 1976, 107 references in 1990, and 2,624 by 1994. In fact, "rite of passage" is used to describe dozens of activities as different as piercing a nose to induction into the military.

This expanding use of the term coincides with increasing uneasiness over the difficulty of growing up in America. There may be a connection. In spite of the absurd variety of uses of "rite of passage," there are underlying patterns.

Underlying Patterns: Clues About Growing Up

Take a look at the kinds of experiences called rites of passage. Typically they have to do with alcohol, drugs, cigarettes, and sex. First-time experiences with activities usually considered adult are a threshold the young are anxious to cross. Also considered as rites of passage are the driver's license and keys to the car, military induction and training, the first job, the SAT, the senior prom, graduation from high school and/or college, games of danger such as chicken, tracking, computer hacking, arrest and jail, teenage pregnancy, and initiation into a gang.

What are the characteristics of these experiences that lead writers to call them "rites of passage"? Despite some overlap, the following are aspects to consider in thinking about the impact of so-called "rite-of-passage" experiences on the young: challenge, setting, relationships, role, responsibility, power and autonomy, knowledge and skill, self perception, and status. Let's take a look at them.

These experiences called "rites of passage" all represent *challenge*, often a risk, a "call to adventure." As dangerous as tracking is—jumping down onto a subway track, running ahead of the train and jumping out mere seconds before being run down—it is a way of taking on a challenge and proving courage in the eyes of one's peers. For lack of anything more promising to do, it is a response to the call to adventure. So too is going to prison. The *Washington Post* (6/24/90) comments that "[s]ome see prison time as a 'rite of passage,' or a 'badge of courage,' which wins attention from family and peers, albeit negative attention." [1]

Such experiences often involve a *new setting* in which to operate. Going off to join the Army or Navy is a sure way to find a new setting for one's life, as is getting arrested and going to jail. Even the shopping mall, as the *Los Angeles Times* (1/6/91) describes it, is a new setting for operation: "Hangouts [at the mall] have become as much of a rite of passage for teen-agers as braces and Clearasil." *Investor's Daily* (11/1/90) suggests another setting, the beach: "Spring break, that ubiquitous rite of passage for so many college students, is big business for firms that market their products to the younger generation."

New relationships come with new settings, particularly where a community of peers is involved. Whether it is life in a college dorm or patrolling the streets in a gang, the new network of relationships becomes critically important. *Newsday* (11/4/90) gives a telling commentary on social relationships: "[B]eating and robbing gays seemed almost like sport to these young men—a thrilling brutal rite of passage. On that April night the young men rode around the neighborhood and even stopped at a deli for refreshments."

A *new role* is often taken on which involves new tasks. Certainly the job at the local Safeway or GAP opens up a new identity—beyond that of son, daughter, or student—for the high school youngster. The *Boston Globe* (12/3/89) comments that "the rite of passage into the teenage work culture had more to do with gaining independence than forsaking school for monetary rewards."

New responsibilities or obligations come with the new role, even if they are totally inappropriate. In contemporary culture a striking, if sadly inappropriate, self-imposed rite entailing a host of new responsibilities is teenage parenthood. A *Washington Post* (1/22/91) survey of out-of-wedlock births and theories for their cause suggests that parenthood for underclass teenagers, given the lack of other options, is their only perceived way to become adults.[2] This situation will likely continue until other options become available and there is a corresponding shift in behavior.

Such experiences lead to an expanded sense of *power* and *autonomy*. Possession of a baby, a car, a college degree, or, with growing—and alarming—frequency today, a gun, increases one's sense of power. And the guns aren't necessarily illegal or found on the streets. *U.S. News & World Report* (5/8/89) points out in an article on the meaning of guns for the middle class: "For men in particular, guns evoke a near mystical return to their youths, swathed in memories of standing alongside their fathers in dawn-lighted blinds. . . . Guns provide rites of passage for daughters as well as sons."

These activities often imply access to privileged *knowledge* and/or *skill*, traditionally reserved for adults. Driving a car literally opens up a whole new world based on a young person's skill in handling the machine coupled with adequate directional knowledge. Implied in the privilege of driving is a recognition of the self-discipline and emotional maturity sufficient to the responsibility. Such maturity usually comes with greater age. For good reason, some would say, many European countries delay granting drivers' licenses until the age of eighteen. Furthermore, knowledge and skill sought by youth may be as sophisticated as computer hacking or as primal as sexual intercourse. In spite of the fact that such knowledge and skill are often developed—or usurped—by immature youngsters, there is good reason for their traditionally privileged adult possession: Knowledge and skill without parallel responsibility are risky indeed, often deadly to the community at large.

All of the above bring about a *new perception* of the self. The youth's world has moved beyond the home and into a wider arena. The new self-image is often accentuated by a uniform, a new name, a new hairdo or a tattoo. Author Sol Yurick provides a vivid description of this process within the street gang in an interview in *Newsday* (10/9/90): "When young street men form into gangs, they establish symbols of that rite of passage into manhood: There are sometimes fearsome oaths of allegiance, always secret insider slang, the wearing of certain styles of clothes, gold ornaments . . ."

Another essential aspect is recognition by others of *new status*. Perhaps the most widely recognized signs of status for the teenager in America is the driver's license. As a journalist in the *San Francisco Chronicle* (10/11/90) put it, "Getting his driver's license outpassed either of the other rites of passage [registering to vote or studying for the driving test] by a mile." On the other hand, a sign of status for some young women is the debutante ball. The *Los Angeles Times* (9/12/90) comments in an article about a debut for young Chinese women, "But the central vision of any debutante program is still this hallowed rite of passage: the night of the debut extravaganza where the girls are formally introduced to society."

So what do these underlying patterns of experiences called rites of passage mean? They seem to point to some kind of transformation—moving from one stage of life to the next, one set of attitudes and behavior to another. Most of them imply moving toward adulthood, however distorted that movement may be.

If we look *only* at the mass media characterizations of rites of passage, we see that they are predominantly negative, not particularly growth-inducing, and are as likely to lead toward jail as they are toward maturity. In the absence of community-guided customs, the term "rite of passage" has become a metaphorical net, cast at random, but failing as often as succeeding to catch relevant experiences. We seem to be groping for apt activities to match a seemingly significant label. At this point in American public awareness, "rite of passage" is a concept in search of a reality.

The search for the reality is critical because it promises clues to the complexity of the maturing process in the human species. Insights can speak to the crisis of youth caught in a nether land of immaturity. Certainly a society as sophisticated as ours has something better to offer its young people than leaving them alone to struggle through aborted attempts to grow up with negative "rites of passage." The idea that an isolated youth has to make the passage from adolescence to adulthood as best as possible without the support and guidance of the whole community is an anomaly in the human experience.[3]

Tribal Rites: Clues About Growing Up

For millennia tribal and religious rites of passage have directed youth on the path to adulthood. Cultures have almost universally troubled themselves with providing rituals of transformation for their young—the expense, the time, the resources. Why? What was the compelling need?

How were such rites structured? Why did they work? But wait a minute, what are rites of passage anyway?

The term, "rite of passage," originated in the work of anthropologist Arnold van Gennep in his 1909 book *Les rites de passage*.[4] The label may have been new but hardly the reality for which it stood. The reality, as van Gennep discovered in his cross-cultural research, was the universal experience of life crises and the web of ritual and ceremony which surrounds them. So rituals were enacted, both to set in motion these necessary transitions and to provide a safety zone for the resulting transformations. Rites of passage for coming-of-age were often highly dramatic performances of symbolic death and rebirth. They often entailed the painful alteration of the body: removal of or filing the teeth, patterned scarring of the skin or tattooing, pulling the hair out, circumcision or clitoridectomy.[5]

This is pretty heavy stuff, but the transformation it was meant to evoke was not to be taken lightly. Survival of the community depended on a mechanism effective in helping the young release their lives as children in order to take on their new lives as adults. Childish attitudes and behavior often were literally and always symbolically cut away. Traditional communities could not afford the luxury of members who were takers and not contributors. Everyone had to grow up in order that all could survive.

Van Gennep's 1909 work did not appear in English until 1960. At that point it had had little influence on sociological theory. Yet two decades later, the term had not only caught on in the social sciences but had become popular in the public consciousness.[6] Whereas in the early '60s there was little evidence that American educators recognized the potential for critical learning during such periods of life crisis, tribal wisdom, on the other hand, had seized these times to teach and test the young people—in survival skills, tribal law, mythology—as part of the intense preparation for their new adult roles.

Yet a secularized urban world has as much need for ritualized transition as did tribal cultures studied by van Gennep at the turn of the 20th century.[7] One dimension of mental illness may be related to the increasing number of individuals who "are forced to accomplish their transitions alone and with private symbols."[8] Adjustments to new stages of life are as much cultural as they are biological phenomena; they need the social mechanisms provided by a healthy culture to ensure the safe and harmonious shift in status.

A certain amount of disorder, especially of young males, goes with adolescent coming of age in any human community. What cushions and celebrates these periodic disturbances in contemporary life? Getting blasted at a fraternity party? Going to the prom? Joining a gang? Hosting a sweet sixteen party? Undergoing a bar or bat mitzvah? Confirmation? Does anyone know?

If tribal cultures had not created social structures to channel the process, community survival—at best precarious—would have been even more endangered. Social philosophers warn, ". . . [E]very society must be wary of the unattached male, for he is universally the cause of numerous social ills."[9]

In tribal cultures the whole community is involved in the process of guiding the young to maturity. By its very nature, a tribal culture depends on the contribution of every member to the survival and well-being of the whole group. If there are individuals who are immature, incompetent, and non-contributive—consumers only rather than producers—they are an obvious drain on the whole. No small community can afford this kind of burden. Therefore, a mechanism is essential for training and ensuring that the young are ready for moving definitively into maturity at the appropriate time.

Stages. That movement is achieved in stages, which reveal an underlying pattern in the rites of passage: separation, transition, and incorporation.[10] *Separation* sets the rite in motion. For the young male, separation from the world of the mother is essential on the path to manhood; inappropriate attachment represents dependency.[11] Male initiation most often takes place apart from the village in groups of peers under the leadership of the older males of the tribe, the elders. Female separation, on the other hand, is more frequently a solitary experience for the girl, usually at the time of her first menstruation, but still under the guidance of the older women of the tribe. Her separation from the community at this time provides her with relief from community tasks and with the solitude to reflect on the changes in her body and to learn the ways and beliefs of the women.[12]

For both—male and female—there is a ritual rip from juvenile dependence, a social shove to independence, and a powerful pull toward interdependence, at first with age cohorts and adult mentors and guides, later with the community at large. The rip, the shove, the pull: the community is planning, guiding, and executing the whole process. Transition at this time is inevitable; there is no turning back.

The second stage, the *transition* or *transformation* phase, may last a few minutes; it may last several years. Transition stages upset the status quo. They are always considered dangerous. The stage between adolescence and adulthood is usually spent in seclusion from the community. Girls learn the ways of the women, boys, the ways of the men. The reality they held as children must be re-framed into the reality appropriate to adulthood.

Anthropologist Victor Turner calls the second stage of a rite of passage the liminal stage, from the Latin *limen* for "threshold," indicating a kind of psychological and spiritual threshold "betwixt and between" what one was and what one will become.[13] This is the phase of creativity and possibility, a place of sheer potentiality. When young initiates are in this stage they are sacred and set apart, usually physically as well as emotionally, from normal home life.[14] Their prior habits of feeling, thinking, and acting are stripped away. Thus they are in a highly suggestible state for learning because they are cut off from the usual ways of perceiving the world.

Entry into "sacred space" demanded by the liminal period may in one way be like the time some American youth spend in the Job Corps or in college. Both experiences can provide the liminal space for transformation to happen, but more often they do not. Why? Perhaps because American culture has as yet no clear concept of what kind of transformation should take place, except into that of a consumer.[15]

The kind of learning, however, which takes place during a rite of passage is totally unlike that of the classroom. The ritual is performance as much as pedagogy, theater more than academics. The method often involves masks and images, music and dance.[16] "Monsters" created in ritual drama are not so much to terrorize or entertain the initiates but, rather, to force them to think about what they have taken for granted in their environment: all assumptions are challenged. Reflection like this is essential to the liminal phase.

In tribal cultures, if initiates have participated fully in the ritual, they enter the third stage and are *incorporated*

16

into the world of the adults. At that point the transition is complete. The community celebrates with them their new identity and new role. Initiates take up their lives as transformed human beings, bringing with them the appropriate perspective, behavior, and skills of an adult to the life of the community.

Implications for 21st Century Youth

So what does all of this have to do with the kids on the streets of L.A.'s East Side, Chicago's West Side, or D.C.'s Southeast? If we are to believe the mass media, the kids are going out and inventing their own rites of passage. The impulse toward the journey to adulthood is so powerful that our young people will create their own paths one way or another. Teenagers find a way to grow up: not always healthy but certainly heroic.

If we compare the "rites" described in the media with the rites described by the anthropologists, we can recognize some superficial similarity. Van Gennep's model involves separation, transition, and incorporation. Whether a youth goes off to college, to jail, or into the Army, each of the experiences would qualify as entry into a symbolic rite of passage. However, there may or may not be an emotional separation from home. Furthermore, each of the experiences—college, jail, Army—involves some kind of orientation during which a transition to a certain set of attitudes and behavior is expected to occur. But that shift may or may not happen. Finally, in each situation, the "initiate" is expected to return at some point to "normal" life as a transformed human being who will bring back knowledge important both to the self and to the community.

Ultimately, the critical question is what kind of transformation has taken place in the process? If the young person has truly taken on the perspective and behavior of a mature adult, the experience was indeed a rite of passage. If, on the other hand, the "initiate" returns with immature attitudes, dependency, and egocentric behavior patterns, then the rite has not "taken," and the individual and the community will have to bear the consequences.

Reflections

Key ideas emerge from reflection on tribal rites which have serious relevance for moving into adulthood, no matter what the era of history or what the cultural backdrop:

- the importance of cutting away childish attitudes and behavior in order to take on attitudes and behavior more befitting the new stage of life;

- the importance of focusing attention and energy of both the initiates and the community at large on what is happening in the life of the young person and how it contributes to the well-being of the whole community;

- the importance of taking advantage of a critical learning stage for imparting culturally important knowledge, values, and skills, especially honing survival skills;

- the importance of developing the ability to reflect, which makes possible considered action rather than primal reaction—that is, the capacity for higher order thinking and behaving, and finally;

- the importance of learning the story or stories of the community, the social glue, the structure on which community members "hang" their experiences in order to make sense of them.

A New Rite Emerging. In the context of a *true* rite of passage, media allusions to "rites of passage" often demean the concept of coming-to-maturity. These references, however, are not all superficial. Out of this complex mix of metaphors, there is a clue to something which may spur the evolution of public awareness regarding the coming-of-age in America. If we carefully read the public commentary on youth, we find a suggestion that deserves thorough and thoughtful consideration. It may be the clue to what anthropologists have said is missing from American culture: an effective rite of passage for contemporary youth.

In contrast to tribal rites—meant to ensure the status quo—a new kind of rite is emerging in American culture. A significant experience that could trigger the passage to maturity may well be a youth service experience. Harris Wofford, former senator of Pennsylvania who participated in the founding of the Peace Corps in 1961 and of AmeriCorps in 1994, became in 1995 the CEO of the Corporation for National and Community Service. He said in '94, "I would love to see service—whether community service or service overseas—as a common expectation for young people, a routine rite of passage."[17]

Such socially-supported experiences at that critical juncture of life—late teens, early 20s—may have the kind of transforming effect that traditional rites of passage have ensured, and yet be immediately relevant to the times and needs of the present human community.

To determine, however, whether youth service qualifies as an genuine rite of passage, we must explore whether it fulfills the function of a rite of passage—that is, does it transform an adolescent into an adult? To find out, we draw from several perspectives: our understanding of tribal cultures, discussed in this chapter; the clues found in religious traditions, described in Chapter Two; and the insights found in developmental psychology, discussed in Chapter Three. But most important are the experiences of those who have themselves moved into adulthood through a youth service experience. Their stories, in Chapters Four, Five, and Six, point out ways in which youth corps experiences at this juncture can transform lives.

Something significant is struggling to birth in American culture: a new institution to help young people grow up. The time may soon come when the right of passage into adulthood will be through the rite of passage of voluntary youth service.

* * *

Chapter Two

Traditional Rites:
How Do We Get the Kids to Grow
Up?

Every parent who has endured adolescence with his or her offspring has wondered, How do we get the kids to grow up? Parents in tribal and traditional religious and ethnic communities have not only wondered the same thing but have worked together to ensure that the kids would indeed grow up. As the African proverb goes, "It takes a whole village to raise a child."[1] The idea that young people should flounder around without the help of the whole community as they try to make the journey from adolescence to adulthood is a certain invitation to chaos.

The attempt to grow up on the street, as the daily news indicates, is a disaster.[2] On the other hand, young Americans who are fortunate enough to go to college may grow up in the process, but the collegiate experience does not guarantee maturity.[3] Anyone who has spent a week in a college dorm or fraternity house might believe just the opposite.

Research from the past 20 years on the impact of college on young people gives us an important message.

The personal characteristics students bring with them to college have a critical bearing on the quality of their collegiate experience. This implies that something significant has to happen to the young person before or apart from or parallel to the college experience. What is it then that can help develop and enhance these special qualities?

If adulthood were merely a matter of chronological maturation, parents could simply grit their teeth and stick it out for a decade or so. But when 20-year-olds are being shot before they have a chance at adulthood; when 25-year-olds come home[4] and expect mom to do the laundry and dad to buy the groceries; when 30-year-olds are drifting because they lack a sense of direction in life; and when 40-year-olds still respond to the machismo of street gangs, the neo-Nazis, and the militia, a signal of cultural distress should be going up. We must do something! But what?

The overview of tribal rites of passage in Chapter One indicates what rituals should accomplish, both in the young initiate and in the whole community. Stone-age peoples had a vested interest in the safe passage of their young into the next stage of life; each member had to play a role in the survival of the whole.

As societies developed and changed, new institutions grew up to prepare the young for adulthood. Western culture marked the passage of males into adulthood primarily through military organization and/or apprenticeship in the guilds, and, for some youths, through monastic training.[5] The markers of adulthood for young women who did not enter religious life were marriage and childbirth. The medieval and post-medieval world fused secular and sacred rituals; religious symbol and ceremony marked the entry into the military, the monastery, the state of marriage, and the guild.

22

On the other hand, the fully secularized[6] industrial life of late 19th and early 20th century Western culture invited both young men and young women into adulthood by putting them to work—in the coal mines, the garment district, the steel mills, the telephone switchboard and the meat-packing plants—and working them to exhaustion. Machines replaced apprenticeships. Industries exploited cheap youthful labor.[7]

Post-industrial America still faces the formidable task of transforming its young people. Yet we lack the comprehensive work and social structures—except for a few school-to-work programs—to bring them into adult life. Germany, on the other hand, is a model of a broad apprenticeship program, which provides a bridge from secondary school into the world of work.[8]

Achieving adulthood, however, is more than simply a matter of moving into a good job, as worthy as that might be. In addition to job skills, young people must discover their connection to the broader community and the role they must play in it. In order to bring young people to that realization, a number of other cultures, both European and non-European, provide youth service programs as the expected transition from school to work and adulthood.[9] And here in the United States and abroad, traditional religious and ethnic communities continue to reaffirm the spiritual connection of their youth to their communities through religious rites, usually around the time of puberty.

Religious Rites: Sacrament, Ceremony, Celebration

What can we learn in a secular age like ours, from traditional religious rites of passage as we search for appropriate journeys to adulthood? What possible clues are present in religious rituals, especially when marketing meccas such as teen Celebrations Expos in New York City tout the social support and resources for such events together with sweet-sixteen parties?[10] What does it mean when young ladies' dresses for $150 and party entertainment such as gold robots for $1,200 a night, dee-jays, karaoke, light shows, and video games become the focus of attention; when the memories of those looking back at their coming-of-age revolve around their "take" rather than their transformation? Has the secular swallowed up the sacred, the ceremony, the sacrament?

The fact is that for Christians and Jews in the United States the "rituals of adulthood"—confirmation and *bar* and *bat mitzvah*—are important enough to spend millions in dollars and hours of preparation. Such events deserve attention because they demand attention—certainly within their respective communities.

Yet they usually occur a decade before the typical student graduates from college or trade school and tend often to be more social than spiritual events.[11] The youngsters return to their seventh or eighth grade classrooms and resume life as usual, at least as far as the world at large is concerned. They lose the awareness of a spiritual transformation as math and English classes resume and playground rivalries revive. Life goes on, seemingly, the same as before. Unless—and this is an important point—unless the community now includes the youngster in its religious participation in a way that is decidedly different than what he or she experienced before the ritual.

Many religious communities have found ways to ease their children into religious participation. Catholics introduce their youngsters to the sacrament of the Eucharist, or Holy Communion, around the age of six or seven. Furthermore, they encourage their children to make sacrifices for Lent—the 40-day preparation for Easter— perhaps give up something they enjoy such as candy or TV and observe the abstinence from meat on Fridays.

Muslims introduce their children to the partial practice of fasting at the age of nine during *Ramadan* (a month the Muslims consider the holy season when adults must fast during the daylight hours). For three years within an observant Islamic community, the children fast on weekends during *Ramadan*. By the age of 12, the young Muslim is ready to take on the adult duty of fasting for the whole month.

Jewish parents introduce their children to fasting at *Yom Kippur*. At first they fast for part of the day starting around age 10. But somewhere between the age of 12 and 16, they fast for the full day, beginning the evening before and continuing until that day's nightfall.

Each of these practices introduces children to spiritual and physical discipline. It not only reinforces their religious and ethnic identity within a community beyond the family, but also gives them practice in controlling their own impulses, an element essential to becoming an adult.

Jewish *Bar/Bat Mitzvah*

The terms *bar* and *bat mitzvah* refer both to the youngsters involved as well as to their coming-of-age ritual.[12] The literal meaning is "son or daughter of the commandment," in other words, a person subject to the commandments (*mitzvoth*). But popular usage connects the terms to the ceremony through which the youngster becomes responsible for observing the laws of Judaism and therefore takes on the moral responsibility for his or her own behavior. Up to this point the parents had that responsibility.

The community traditionally invites the boy to formal participation in the worship service. The precise form of religious participation can vary. It may be to create and offer an original prayer. It may be to read from the *Torah* in Hebrew. It may be to discuss a theme from scripture or the law.[13] A meal or party marks the event.

Bat mitzvahs came into common use following World War II in the Conservative, Reconstructionist, and Reform branches of Judaism.[14] The nature of the girl's participation depends on the individual community. Usually the less orthodox the community, the more egalitarian the *bar* and *bat mitzvahs* tend to be, sometimes becoming indistinguishable from each other.

Confirmation became a part of Reform Judaism in 19th century Germany as an alternative to *bar mitzvah*. Girls and boys together participated in a group ceremony on or near the festival of *Shavu'ot* (the celebration of the reception and acceptance of the *Torah*, the Law). Because it represented their commitment to Judaism at the age of 16 or 17, it was more properly a coming-to-adulthood milestone.

In the United States confirmation continued to be part of the Reform Jewish youngster's experience of growing up. The coming of the 1950s and '60s, however, reintroduced the bar and bat mitzvah to Reform congregations. On the other hand, confirmation became part of some Conservative and Reconstructionist congregations' experience.

Sharon, a 24-year-old VISTA volunteer, recalls her coming-of-age experience in Judaism and the dilemma she faced because her family belonged to a Conservative synagogue and she attended an Orthodox school.

> I did not have a *bat mitzvah*. . . . While my synagogue allowed it, I was afraid to have all these kids from school see me doing the "less correct" thing, as I perceived it at the time.
>
> So I did something different. Since I was born in the summer time [the *bar* and *bat mitzvah* are held as close to the birthday as possible], we went to Israel. We got to know about the culture that way. I chose a Biblical passage that is part of the prayers for the day I was born, "Hear, O Israel, the Lord is our God." Martyrs usually say it when they're being killed. The *bar* and *bat mitzvah* custom is to give a brief talk about the meaning of this passage in your life. To tell the truth, I don't remember what I said. It was a long time ago.
>
> We shared the event with a friend of mine on the terrace of the King David Hotel, . . . overlooking the Wailing Wall and the Old City—a phenomenal view. We had morning services with a rabbi who was in Israel for the summer. We each said our little sermons and had brunch afterwards. My friend, our families, and anyone we knew who happened to be in Israel that summer were there. Looking back on it, it was very nice. It was small and simple. That was in August of 1982.
>
> When I came back from Israel and went back to school, I don't remember feeling significantly different. For a boy, I think, it's slightly different in that it's the first time he puts on a *tefillin* . . . this small black box [strapped to the forehead] which contains the prayer that I was talking about earlier. He also puts on the prayer shawl for the first time. He stands before the

27

congregation. I think it's much more transformational, even if it's just with physical objects. With girls, it's not like you've received anything new. They don't put on a prayer shawl . . . although some do now.

I'm reaching an age now when I'm following religious laws because I want to, not because my parents want me to. Because I grew up at a religious school, we prayed every day. So it was kind of a big part of my life anyway. It may have been different if I had not been raised with religion so much a part of my life, and suddenly this big ceremony [the bat mitzvah] is coming upon me. I think it would have been much harder to learn Hebrew. Because of my school, there were a lot of things I already knew. It wasn't quite as traumatic . . . but it wasn't quite as much of a transformation either.

I was raised with a family that was very service-oriented. I was raised to believe that you should look beyond your own nose. There are other people out there that you should worry about. Our teachers would talk about the Ten Commandments being on two tablets. On one side are all the things having to do with God, the other side with people. They are equal. Neither side is bigger than the other, and neither is more important. Even the ideal underlying *Yom Kippur* is that you can't be a good Jew and not a good person. In that sense, service has always been part of my growing up.

It's very common in Jewish families to send their older children to Israel for a year. In high school they tried to convince us to go to Israel during that year between high school and college to get us more steeped in religion and convert us. My father, still—when I have the time off between VISTA and going back to grad school—he keeps telling me that I should go to Israel.

28

In Canada, as well, Jewish parents are seeking an effective way to imprint their children with a sense of their religious identity. Despite concerns for their children's safety in the dangerous political climate of Israel, many Canadian parents send their children to their spiritual homeland. The *Toronto Star* (8/3/90) comments,

> The Israel trips have become a rite of passage. They can spark a sense of Jewish identity often blurred by life as an assimilated minority in Canada.

What becomes evident in the Jewish experience is that enormous resources are brought to bear on imprinting the young with an identity within their ethnic and religious community, and that often involves a tie to the geographical homeland.

Christian Rituals

During the time of industrialization in Germany there was no question about the meaning of the sacrament of confirmation. The young men who went neither to the university to become scholars nor to the fields to become farmers ended their formal education at the age of 14 when they were confirmed. This marked their entry into adulthood and meant they could enter apprenticeship.[15]

A Catholic Experience. In contrast to such precise expectation, the debate over the age of confirmation in the American Catholic Church opens up some of the most critical issues regarding rituals of initiation: what they do and what they symbolize. Is confirmation a bridge between childhood and adolescence or a bridge between adolescence and adulthood? Does the sacrament initiate the child into the years of preparation for adulthood, or does it celebrate the end of that preparation as the final symbolic step into the adult faith community?

Some parents in the Milwaukee Diocese, where confirmation is reserved for 16-year-olds, have taken their children to the Peoria Diocese (Illinois) at the age of 11 to be confirmed. These parents fear that if they wait until 16 for confirmation their children may lose interest in the faith. If, on the other hand, they confirm early, they believe they will reinforce their children's identity as young Catholics and thus keep them in the church.[16] A director of a national Catholic association in Washington, D.C., reflects on the changes:

> During the '70s—probably as a result of the Vatican II Council—there was a renewal of liturgical and sacramental practice. In coming to grips with the need for deepening spiritual and developmental experiences for youth, as well as for other reasons, the Church in many dioceses decided to raise the age of reception of the sacrament of confirmation to 14, 15, or 16. The traditional age had been 10. For example, I was confirmed when I was 10-years-old.

> The age of 15 or 16 is a relatively new practice in the United States—and a debated practice. More than 50% of the parishes in the country now probably celebrate the sacrament of confirmation between the ages of 13 and 16. . . . We're trying to come to grips with initiation and conversion—because what we're talking about here is conversion. How do we help children, young people, young adults, change their ways and, in a sense, follow the way of the Christ?

> Community service is now an expectation. Most programs that have trained personnel and a community commitment realize and acknowledge the need to

engage and involve young people in forms of service. I think initially people viewed service as something nice, but they may or may not have recognized it as a way of applying one's faith to one's life.

The Presence of God. But something deeper has surfaced since Vatican II [in the 1960s]—actually it has been around for centuries in the Christian tradition—and that is the deep appreciation for social justice, the importance of a social application of our faith. Service is a way of moving toward a heightened awareness of the connection between our personal private faith and the presence of God in our lives, in the community, in one another, in strangers. If I am a Christian, what does this imply in regard to my relation to others? If we're called to live out the Beatitudes, what is the connection here between what I believe and how I act?

When I think back to my own experience of being confirmed as a 10-year-old, I remember that one of the images we were taught was to become a soldier of Christ. This was in a Catholic school setting where most of the focus was on the material content. So here were these war-like images. We were encouraged to go to battle for Christ. At the time—I can't recall directly— but probably some of the ideas of Communism might even have filtered in. [This was during the 1950s.] The school structure was very regimented. Marching and order were important.

Knowledge plus Service. Where did this idea for drawing service into the preparation for confirmation come from? Not everyone accepts it, by any means. We've received a lot of criticism over the past 10 or 15 years from the more traditional believers who focus purely on the doctrinal and cognitive aspects of religious development. What happened in some instances is that one's personal experience of faith and life took precedence over knowledge. We've received criticism from some in the church saying that our young people are illiterate today. They really don't know the basic teachings.

As I reflect upon that, I think there's a certain legitimacy to what they're saying. But when I look at the total picture, and I see these service projects and young people getting involved in communities—the faith community but also the larger community—I don't know if that's a real negative. The ideal, of course, is an integration of the two: knowledge of church teachings and faith experience enhanced by reflective service to the community.

For the Catholic community, the importance of service in the preparation for confirmation and the age of conferral are the big issues right now, both having a bearing on how best to prepare young people for moving into adulthood.

The *Quinceanera* Experience. Hispanic families consider the *quinceanera* (loosely translated, "15 years") far more than the sacrament of confirmation as the rite of passage for their 15-year-old daughters. It has indeed been their entry into the adult world in traditional cultures where it coincides with their termination of girlhood. Marriage and motherhood often follow closely behind.

In the United States many priests are trying to encourage parents to simplify the social aspect of the ritual. Families can go into debt for years to pay for elaborate gowns and parties befitting their sense of this grand event for their daughters, every bit as elegant, often, as wedding celebrations. The cost, as for bar and bat mitzvahs, runs into thousands of dollars, often as much as $10,000.[17] Relatives must come to the rescue of parents in paying the price.

Priests and pastors are concerned that the spiritual element gets buried in the elaborate material preparations.

Some parishes require the *quinceanera* applicants to do community service on a weekly basis for a certain period of time, usually about three months. The service requirement is one way of emphasizing the obligations and responsibilities that the young woman now has to society.[18]

A Lutheran Experience. Lutherans consider confirmation the entry into the social community of the church, according to a representative for a midwestern Lutheran organization. It usually takes place during eighth grade. He recalls his own experience:

> In the Lutheran school we attended, the pastor instructed us for an hour two or three mornings a week. The kids in public school came for instruction on Saturday mornings. In a church where infant baptism is the practice, the Lutherans consider confirmation a way of confirming one's baptism. At the same time the church is confirming that the young person has received the proper instruction to make this kind of decision.
>
> The congregation is responsible for designing the program: for instance, how many years of instruction—sometimes two, sometimes as many as four—who will do the instruction, whether a week of summer camp will be part of the experience.
>
> When I was going through it, we had two years of instruction, no camp, and a public examination by the pastor on the Friday night before the big day. The exam took place in church in front of our parents and relatives. The pastor fired questions at us. It was a rather humiliating experience. Most congregations don't do it that way now. The students are tested privately by

33

whatever means the congregation decides. I think people now think it unnecessary to put that kind of pressure on a kid.

A service requirement is now fairly widespread. Most parents consider it a good way to involve their youngsters in the life of the church. It can take so many forms—from mowing a neighbor's lawn to working on a church committee—that it's hard to object.

Confirmation is seen as crossing the threshold into the adult membership of the church. The confirmants get a box of envelopes and are now expected to contribute financially. They are also expected to commune on a regular basis, usually three or four times a year. And if you are a confirmed member, you are now able to serve on committees of the church, even as a young teenager. So there are expectations and responsibilities.

Not all young Lutherans choose to be confirmed, which was the case with this man's three sons. The choice is deliberate and demands a commitment to the instruction and service requirements.

Even more demanding in the larger religious world, however, is the choice to enter a consecrated life of service as a member of the clergy or sisterhood. At one time religious orders took young men and women at the age of 13. This practice is now out of favor. Completion of high school, and even of college, is more the rule now than the exception.

A Nun's Experience. Both the Catholic and the high Episcopal Church invite young women into religious adulthood by offering them the opportunity to devote themselves to a life of spiritual dedication. The way of the sister, or the nun, was traditionally framed by the metaphor of the bride of Christ.

One woman's story, a Roman Catholic sister, now 90-years-old, conveys the dedication of such a life. From young girlhood, Sister Karen felt called to a religious life, often imagining herself going off to Leper Island and dedicating herself to the care of the lepers. A serious illness at the age of 12 and a doctor's warning that her health could not stand such a choice, made her reconsider. As a 17-year-old senior in high school she held to her calling in spite of her attraction to a certain red-headed young man. Following graduation in 1923 she entered the novitiate of a midwestern convent. She recalls,

> In those days young people were making life decisions at the end of high school. So I chose to enter a religious community. Just as the Army has boot camp, so we had boot training, and our headquarters was in Dubuque, Iowa [a long way from my Colorado home]. The sisters had told me, "Oh, you'll love Dubuque. There are hills there that will remind you of the mountains." They didn't remind me of the mountains at all. I was terribly, terribly homesick. I cried for weeks. The lonesomeness was awful.

> At some point, one of the older sisters said, "I thought you were an only child, so I've been feeling sorry for you. I just found out you are one of 10! I'm not going to feel sorry for you anymore." That made me laugh, and I began to get over my loneliness.

> The training period [called the novitiate] let the community see if you had what they wanted and for you to see if that's where you would fit in. We also learned [during this time] to meditate and pray.

> **Vows**. When the time came, I took the three vows of religious life: poverty, chastity, and obedience. Our vows free us not constrain us.

35

In the vow of poverty, you give up all your wealth . . . which I didn't have, so I didn't have to give it up. You also give your mental and your spiritual gifts as well. You dedicate them entirely to the work of God by trying to be Christ-like in this world. Having this kind of poverty frees us from wanting to be wealthy. Those of us engaged in intellectual work, it frees us from wanting to be prominent. It frees us to respond to the real needs of the world.

The second vow is chastity. I am convinced that no person becomes a fully developed adult unless they have had a very deep love affair or commitment, either to a person or to a cause. It's a matter of the heart. No love grows unless it's fed, and that's as true in religious life as it is in marriage. Almost every girl I knew [in the novitiate with me] told me, "You know, I was really in love with a man, but Christ kept calling to me."

I remember on a Holy Thursday begging God to give me a vocation. I was running after Him. He wasn't running after me. All these other girls said God was pursuing them. I felt kind of cheated. In just the last few years someone said to me, "How did you resolve that?" I finally decided that this desire [to give myself to Christ] had come from God because it couldn't have come from anywhere else. That gave me a bit of peace about it.

Obedience is the third vow. There are two kinds of obedience. There is obedience from the top down: God tells the superior what you should do and then you do it. That's a childish way. The more adult way is to find out by prayer and discernment what God's will is for you in what you are doing. Does your will correspond with that?

Choices. Here is an example of how my vow of
obedience worked in my life: By the end of our novitiate
we had taken just a few college courses. I would have
chosen to study drama or English or Latin. I was very
good in those. But they needed math teachers. So Karen
studied math . . . to meet the need. I chose to give my
life completely, and this was part of that choice.

[At the end of novitiate] I was sent to a large urban high
school to teach. I brought a wonderful high school
background: four years of Latin, four years of math, four
years of science. In addition, I had those few college
courses in the novitiate.

I was assigned to a sophomore homeroom where I had
to teach religion, English, biology, and geometry. I went
to the principal and said, "I do not know enough to teach
these girls." She said, "Oh, you think you're in the
wrong place, that you don't have a vocation?" Well, that
shocked me, so I went in and did it. The older sisters
were wonderful about giving me suggestions. They were
mentors for us.

I was only 19 when I went to teach high school. I taught
high school for 18 years. Then I was sent to [an urban
women's] college. By that time I had my degrees in
math and became head of the math department and dean
of admissions.

The president of the student council that year, an
unusually mature student, said, "Sister Karen, don't you
let a week go by without touching the lives of the poor
in some way." So every Saturday for years I went to the
inner city to work with the people to improve their
situation in the city. I never thought of being afraid. I
simply went by myself on the rapid transit. I took that
student's admonition to me very seriously.

Since retiring from active teaching, Sister Karen has continued to tutor reluctant math students, especially young women. She stays in touch with alumni from the college, offering love and encouragement to those going through difficult times. She makes a point of auditing several courses a year and keeping up with current events and theological issues. As she reflects on her long life of service, she muses, "I have come to know that God actually loves us into existence. My life is a gift."

Islam

First generation Muslim teenagers and their parents face a special challenge in trying to maintain their religious faith and identity within a culture that is for the most part unsympathetic. Parents find themselves walking a tightrope in seeking the right balance between lax discipline and low expectations on the one hand and rigidity and authoritarianism on the other. Sahib, a young business executive in a large midwestern city, recalls growing up Muslim in American suburbia:

> My parents were reasonably strict. A lot of parents are
> unreasonably strict, and then the kids end up drinking
> and dating and sleeping around when they go to college
> even though their parents are some of the most religious
> people in the country. These kids were never given
> flexibility and freedom.
>
> Other kids are given a ton of freedom but not taught
> what's right and wrong. The parents have no idea what
> the kids are doing. Some of the girls who cover their
> hair and go to the mosque, when they go to college their
> hair's uncovered and they are out partying. My parents
> taught us a lot, but they also gave us enough freedom at

an early age to the point when I got to college, I wasn't tempted because I had seen it all in high school anyway. There wasn't this big apple sitting right in front of me that I hadn't seen before.

Moving Toward Adulthood. It's hard to say when you become an adult in the religion. Some of the adult responsibilities, like fasting and praying, are expected of you when you are a young teenager. By the time most children are 8 to 10-years-old, they have read the *Qur'an*. That's a kind of rite of passage. You are supposed to become fluent in reading it. Kids study and they practice. They memorize and they learn and they read.

There's not really a ceremony like a *bar mitzvah* or confirmation or something like that in Islam. Anywhere from 9 to 13-years-old, children are introduced to fasting. It depends on the individual, what community he and she are living in, and how mature they are physically. A lot of kids do it automatically because all of their friends are doing it.

I think my first fast was in fourth grade. I did it maybe two or three times that month. For a lot of kids when they keep their first fast, that evening the parents throw a party for them, but that is more of a cultural than a religious thing.

By the time you are 13 or 14, you should be praying five times a day—it's required. Most students graduate from Sunday School between ninth and tenth grade, around the age of 15 or 16. You attend the service and prayers. You become an assistant teacher. You're in youth activities. You're taking on new responsibilities.

Responsibilities. When you are an adult in Islam, you must follow five tenets: Every Muslim has to acknowledge *Allah*—"There is no God but *Allah* . . . and Mohammed is his messenger"; pray five times a day; give 2.5 percent of your net savings to charity; fast during the month of *Ramadan* from sunrise to sunset, and then there's the pilgrimage to Mecca. Each person is supposed to make that pilgrimage as an adult. "Adult" in this case is when you can support yourself. If you cannot afford to go, you are exempted. If you are a woman, you have to have a male companion go with you.

My own feeling of becoming an adult happened during my last year of high school when my parents had to move [out of the country because of their jobs]. I chose to stay and finish that final year in my American high school. I lived with family friends but was also taking care of the family house.

The tenants walked out and left it damaged. I had to work with the real estate agent to deal with it. That's when I knew I was an adult. But that was more of a situational thing than an age or religious thing. My parents and family were depending on me . . . not just me depending on myself.

What becomes evident from Sahib's story on the personal level is the significance of his taking on a role where others depended on him. On the social level is the importance of finding a healthy interchange between the religious and secular communities. Ideally, they should reinforce, rather than conflict with, each other in bringing the young to maturity.

African-American Initiatives

During the summer of 1982 the National Urban League released a report by sociologist Bruce Hare, entitled "The Rites of Passage: A Black Perspective."[19] The youth development monograph drew attention to the crisis of young African-American males by putting the emergency into a social context. All young people need both the training and the opportunity to make a healthy transition into adulthood. The training depends on adequate education to ensure mental readiness; but equally important is the opportunity for employment.

If the sign of adulthood is the ability to care for oneself and to care for those entrusted to our care, then the mechanism—employment—must be in place to do so. The absence of adequate employment and the chance to work toward employment bring a loss of respect, the feeling of incompetence, and lack of control over one's life and lead to bitter frustration and anger. The traditional male role as protector and provider is denied him. No wonder young men feel driven to prove their manhood in extreme and destructive ways.

Dr. Hare is quite clear about the responsibility within the African-American community for turning the situation around. He is equally clear, however, about the responsibility of the larger social system which has denied the very mechanism necessary to assume healthy adulthood, namely the training and opportunity to obtain adequate employment.

In the growing concern to save a generation of young black males, African-American men are setting up programs around the country to match adult men with teenage boys. Many of the mentoring programs are based on a religious foundation and make use of "traditional

41

African rituals and principles to mark stages of growth and development."[20]

Rite-of-Passage Programs. Since the 1980s a number of Rite-of-Passage programs have grown up in churches, schools, and community agencies. The churches realize that the African rites of passage offer a metaphor for American youth to prove their manhood and womanhood. A program at the Progressive Life Center in Washington, D.C., like other African-American Rites-of-Passage programs around the country, works at instilling a new value system by using the seven African principles: *Umoja* (unity), *Kujichagulia* (self-determination), *Ujima* (collective work and responsibility), *Ujamaa* (cooperative economics), *Nia* (purpose), *Kuumba* (creativity), *Imani* (faith). The D.C. program has added an eighth principle, *Heshema* (respect).[21]

The program begins to teach these principles in fourth or fifth grade and continues to reinforce them at least through junior high school. Rituals, based on African models, provide the young people with a sense of identity and belonging. In many of the programs each of the children receives an African name based on a special quality they possess, usually chosen by the leaders with the advice of the parents. The African principles emphasize to the children a sense of loyalty, responsibility, and self-worth.

The Nation of Islam. One cannot look at programs to "save a generation of young African-American males" without commenting on the importance of Islam in the rite-of-passage process. Since the 1930s, the Fruit of Islam has trained and educated young men and the Muslim Girls the young women.[22] Islam has been especially effective in the jails and prisons.

Alex Haley's *The Autobiography of Malcolm X* is a powerful description of a spiritual transformation, possible even in the most oppressive circumstances. The core of spirituality for Islam, just as it is for all effective religions, is the movement out of an egocentric position toward one of responsibility, self-discipline, and compassion. Islam offers a way of moving toward that reality by transcending the banality of crime and addiction.

The *"jihad,"* which in popular consciousness is "the holy war" and sometimes considered a justification for terrorism, is at a deeper level the lifelong struggle with the lower part of the self.[23] What Islam does is to raise this struggle to the level of conscious commitment, which is what every authentic religion must do.

The Journey as a Metaphor for Coming to Maturity

Malcolm X's pilgrimage to Mecca was symbolic of the journey that all of us are called to take. While in one sense it was a geographical pilgrimage, at a deeper level it was a journey beyond his religious and racial identity toward a conscious connection with all human beings. This was an ultimate heroic journey because he paid for it with his life.

What is apparent, both in Malcolm's prison experience and his pilgrimage to Mecca and in Sister Karen's journey to her Iowa novitiate, is an ancient pattern —the withdrawal and return—found in the lives of all great religious leaders: Moses, Jesus, Mohammed, Siddhartha (Buddha).[24] The withdrawal from ordinary life brings the individual face-to-face with his and her true identity and prepares them to take on their special tasks in life. The return enables the transformed pilgrim to bring back new knowledge and insights to enrich the whole community.

Mythology scholar Joseph Campbell discovered the same basic pattern of withdrawal and return in mythology from all time periods and all cultures.[25] He called this mythic pattern (departure, initiation, and return) "the adventure of the hero." Furthermore, he pointed out that this "hero's journey" parallels the rites of passage as described by the anthropologist Arnold van Gennep as separation, transition, and incorporation.[26]

Nevertheless, whatever words we use to describe the process, it is indeed a "heroic journey," this process of coming to full maturity (or ripeness). Whether we realize it or not, each of us must find our own heroic journey if we would come to adulthood. This is where cultural and religious wisdom can point the way.

Mormon Missionaries

One kind of 'heroic journey"—an expression of religious dedication—is that of the young Mormon missionaries from The Church of Jesus Christ of Latter-day Saints. The Mormon mission experience has long been considered a "rigorous rite of passage."[27] All young men in the church are expected, although not mandated, to serve their two-year mission sometime around the age of 20. Young women are also invited to contribute 18 months at a slightly older age.

Sam remembers his call to the missions in 1960:

You have no control over the mission call. You just put in your papers and say, I'm willing to serve anywhere you want me to serve. Then you wait anxiously for that

44

letter to come that says you have been called to . . . it could be Twin Falls, Idaho . . . it could be Rome, Italy.

Separation. We usually don't call missionaries to serve missions in areas where they live or where they have relatives or family. The church belief is that missionary service is a peculiar service. You dedicate your entire time, life, energy, and resources for those two years to the Lord's work and don't let other things interfere.

So when missionaries go out, they go to that particular mission, and they spend their whole two years there. They don't come home during the two years. Most mission presidents don't allow telephone calls. Families are encouraged to write once a week. Missionaries are encouraged to write home once a week. But no other contact is encouraged. The idea is to separate as much as possible from home and girl friends and family and cars and movies and get away entirely from the life-style of young people to dedicate full attention to this missionary work.

The missionaries always live and work in pairs. The pairs change periodically during the two years. They have no idea who their companion is going to be. For example, if I was called to Spain, I would go to the missionary training center for six weeks to learn Spanish and learn about what I am going to teach, and then I would go from there to Spain where I would be assigned my companion. It would probably be somebody who is already there. You don't want to send two brand new missionaries to the same place at the same time. You want to put one that has some experience with someone that doesn't. So there is a senior companion and a junior companion.

At the end of the two years, if they've served their mission honorably, then it's sort of like being discharged from the military. They receive their letter from their mission president and are sent home.

When they get home, they try to reacclimate themselves to normal life. There is a sociological change that needs to take place during this period. Coming home is a very difficult time. They've had two years of highly dedicated single-purpose work. Now they come back to a world that sometimes has changed in two years, a world they've not had a part of. Remember, they are very young people. They're still just 21-years-old.

Support. When I went out in 1960, there were probably a few thousand missionaries. Today, we're pushing 50 thousand each year. My father said he would support me. The church will pay the transportation out and back, all but $100. The family funds all other support: housing, food, clothing, books, local transportation. If a family can't afford it, there are a lot of people who like to help fund missionaries. In my case, my family paid for my mission, and we're paying for our sons' missions.

So I decided to go. I had a girl friend. That makes it very hard for a young man to say I'm going to leave this girl behind and go for two years. I would say in 90 percent of the cases of the young men that have girl friends, those girl friends are not there when they come home. They will meet someone else—usually a returned missionary. If you're an active LDS young woman, you know that a young man who hasn't served a mission is not really marriage-eligible because he still has a mission to serve. So that is part of the sociology of all this.

Well, I was in that situation, as were both my sons. You have a girl friend. You think that's the person you want to marry, but you can't marry her because you have this

46

church service to fulfill. And I almost didn't go because I didn't want to leave her, and quite frankly she had been dating another fellow who was a missionary and sent him a dear John letter. So I thought, well, it's going to happen to me too.

But after anguishing over that, I decided I would serve as a missionary. I put in my papers. I received my call to the Samoan Islands in the South Pacific. I had to get out an encyclopedia to see where these Samoan Islands were.

Cut Off From the World. I found myself very isolated from the world. The Pan-Am Clipper would come in once a week bringing mail. Then that mail had to go from there by boat to the other islands. So mail was slow and not very frequent. Sometimes several letters would come at once and then nothing for a long while. There were no telephones. There was no other contact with the world.

You could stand just about anywhere and see what was your entire world then. That is, you could see ocean all around you. Just this little place with coconuts and fish and taro and people speaking a funny language, a collection of vowels that I didn't understand.

And you were afraid to eat the food because you thought it was something really weird. There were a lot of cockroaches and mosquitoes. I would sleep in a mosquito net on a grass woven mat on seashells in a thatched roof hut. To take a bath I would wrap a cloth around my waist and stand under a pipe in the middle of the village. It was very primitive . . . clean but very primitive, just basic existence.

I was an emotional wreck in the beginning. The first three months I wanted to come home. I think a lot of

missionaries feel that way. In the States you can get on a
bus or get a car or on a train or plane and go home. I'd
stand on the ocean's edge and look out and see nothing
but water. I couldn't go home. I had to stay there. I was
emotionally isolated. And physically, I needed to learn
to adapt to the humidity and the rain and the bugs and
the food.

Discoveries. Eventually I discovered that the food was
pretty good. But because of the humidity and the
climate, there were a lot of parasites. Not as bad as
South America though. We have a lot of missionaries,
particularly in central America, who get stomach
parasites that bother them the rest of their lives. I did not
have that problem. I was living in an area where we
were drinking surface water, however, and unbeknownst
to me there were some pigs that had been roaming in the
hills above.

I got hepatitis and was out one full month. This was
about midway through my term. By then I fully intended
to stay and finish what I was doing. I had no desire to go
home at that point. In fact, quite the opposite—fearful
that they would send me home. That happens.
Missionaries get illnesses and sometimes do have to be
sent home for treatment. Sometimes they go back to the
mission; sometimes it's a missionary-ending kind of
illness. It's a tragedy for the missionaries.

Many times there are personal tragedies in missionary
lives. Parents die. Brothers and sisters die. And
missionaries will make the decision, based on their need
and their family's needs, whether to stay or not. Life
goes on for the families at home while these
missionaries step away from life. They really separate
themselves entirely—except for letter writing—from
family and friends and everything else about life as they

know it to devote themselves entirely to what they're doing.

Quite frankly, I am grateful that I went to Samoa because maybe I wouldn't have had the emotional constitution to do what I needed to do if I had an escape route. But I was so far removed, and it was such a totally foreign environment.

Our son, who is in Spain now, we have talked to only once in the almost two years he's been gone. His brother and his wife have a year-old baby that he's never seen. He left with his little sister only five; now she's seven. His oldest sister's children, his nephews, are two years older. The missionary misses all that. And the children change the most. So it really is a major sacrifice. The purpose is to serve someone else. Yet the person you serve the most is probably yourself.

Sam returned to the United States to take up his life as an adult. And, yes, he did marry the girl he left behind. From the vantage point of his mid-50s now, he realizes how profoundly the journey marked his life:

What did I learn? I learned to survive. I learned to stick with something, to get it done. I learned to eat different foods. I learned to appreciate other cultures. I learned to respect other people who don't think the same way I do. I learned that I could be deathly ill by myself—that it's okay. What did I learn? I learned maturity.

Reflections

Reflecting on religious rites and experiences imparts a number of lessons:

- The rite of passage for the young person is a conscious entry into the community of faith, which in the case of Christians begins with baptism. The youth experiences a connection to the community: "There is a place for me—I belong."

- The rite represents a commitment to the laws of the religious community. This demands a certain discipline in life style; it may imply fasting, tithing, regular prayer, or dietary prescriptions. "I will follow these laws because this is the price I pay for belonging."

- The religious rites involve the support of the whole community, expressed by its participation, resources, teaching, and celebration. "I must have value because the community is teaching me, participating with me, and celebrating my development."

- The faith community recognizes the rite as a social marker, something conferred at a certain point in life. "I have come of age because my community says I have."

- The rite is a social manifestation of participation in the sacred story. "My experience has value because it tells me something about my relationship with my God and with the people of my community."

When done well, religious rites contribute to the ego identity of the child at puberty. "I belong to this community (religious, racial, ethnic). I will follow its rules; I am valued." Perhaps for this reason, the rites of *bar* and *bat mitzvah* and confirmation are more appropriately conferred at the age of puberty rather than mid to late adolescence.

For if the community strengthens ego-identity at the transition from childhood to adolescence, then young people will be ready to transcend religious, racial, and ethnic barriers at their transition to adulthood. When adolescents have developed a healthy sense of religious, racial, and ethnic identity, they will be less likely to move into adulthood with the anger and rage of those whose identity has been ignored or denigrated as that of young people living by the code of the streets or bearing the burden of ethnic and religious rivalries of a Belfast or a Bosnia.

Limitations of Religious Rites

Where the sacred story is alive, and the rituals have substance and are not empty symbols, the religious rites of passage can carry developmental power. They can be a potent way of imprinting a healthy identity and set of expectations on the young.[28] In spite of signs of an awakening to spiritual concerns, however, contemporary culture still celebrates the cult of narcissism. Materialism for the time being is still winning the upper hand.[29] In such a context rites become mere external observances, excuses for celebration, but devoid of their power to transform. Limitations of the religious rites are evident when viewed against the backdrop of what rites of passage should accomplish:

- To what extent are childish attitudes and behavior cut away when the rituals are conferred on children before they are ready to grow up?

- What is the focus of attention and energy? The special outfit, the entertainment, the gifts? or the spiritual transformation?

- What kind of critical learning is taking place? Rote answers to preprogrammed questions that will slip the mind when the ceremonial outfits are outgrown and the bills are paid?

- To what extent can the ability to reflect be developed when all of the focus is on presentation, entertainment, and celebration?

- To what extent can we enter a sacred story and recognize it as a frame of reference for the rest of our life when the distractions of television, movies, rap music, and the mall are so compelling?

- To what extent does it become apparent that one's own story connects profoundly to that of one's neighbors, when religious instruction focuses only on differences, not similarities, in religious principles and practice?

- To what extent are religious communities, and the public at large, now recognizing the need for appropriate experiences to move the young person into adolescence and others to move him or her out of adolescence and into adulthood? The growing complexity of life and the resulting extension of adolescence point to the need for both.

Symbolic Markers. Yes, religious rites in American culture do have the potential for triggering the journey to adulthood. Yet, because they often focus on the spectacular, material elements, their power to help the kids grow up becomes dissipated. However, when religious practice adds to the ritual an emphasis on spiritual discipline and service, it can reinforce the young person's sense of religious identity and give impetus to maturity. The rites and the rituals then become the symbolic markers and celebrations rather than "magic shows."

Notice how many of the coming-of-age rituals now demand a period of service as a requirement. Notice too a growing concern with the development of character through spiritual initiation. Ritual alone is not enough to transform the young initiate from a child into an adult.

Still, it is significant that some models for youth service as a rite of passage come out of religious practice. The Mormon experience is often held up as an example when a term of service is mentioned as a rite of passage. Young missionaries, although engaged in denominational rather than civic service, must be respected for their courage and spirit of sacrifice, and their endeavor recognized as worthy of earning them adulthood.

Another example initiated within the church should be mentioned in this context. The so-called peace churches —Brethren, Mennonites, and Quakers—had a significant influence on the development of the service corps concept. Their demand for conscientious objection to military combat brought alternate civilian service into being.[30] Their impact is apparent today in the contemporary work camps of the American Friends and the youth corps of the Mennonites and the Brethren. They, in turn, have been models for the Jesuit and the Lutheran Volunteer Corps.[31]

Periodic opinion polls tell us that public awareness is growing regarding the potential of universal service for helping young people come to adulthood in complex times in a complicated society.[32] This is not to suggest that a youth corps experience would replace a religious rite. Rather, it would build on it, recognizing and valuing religious, racial, and ethnic identity, but at the same time transcending it by emphasizing the interconnectedness of *all* people.

We look now at contemporary developmental issues to understand better why it is so difficult for many of our kids to grow up.

* * *

Chapter Three

Contemporary Rites:
Why Are American Kids Postponing Adulthood?

E arlier generations of young people could expect to make their way through the dangers of growing up guided by their religious and mythological symbols and rituals.[1] In late twentieth century America, such dangers are still a part of coming-of-age, now more so than ever. Yet the myths and rituals that traditionally offered guidance are missing or, at best, are available for far too few of our young people.

Tribal cultures offered their young a challenging— but guarded and guided—experience through a symbolic death to rebirth: death to childhood, rebirth to adulthood. Contemporary American youths are undergoing literal death, with no opportunity for rebirth, in their attempts to make their transition. The growing rates of homicide and suicide have turned adolescence into a war zone of life. For too many of our young people the transitional stage is becoming a terminal stage.[2] What's going on here? Young people seem to be falling prey to the seductions of contemporary life: acquisition,[3] addiction and aggression,[4] alienation, and anomie.[5]

Our culture operates under the assumption that material acquisition authorizes adulthood. The driver's license and credit card validate the new identity. The nature of our society at present impels the immature to take possession without taking care; to take power without using intelligence; to choose separation without finding connection; to demand freedom without identifying purpose. The ironic twist is this: Never before have adolescents had the level of privileges that go with adult life—personal income, designer clothes, sexual experience, freedom of transportation—yet never before have they been less prepared to deal with them responsibly.[6]

The difficulty of the journey from adolescence to adulthood shows itself in the growth of literature since the mid-'80s, both on masculine and feminine maturity and on the dependency of adult children.[7] People are reaching mid-life and discovering that they did not experience an effective rite of passage into adulthood. They suffered its absence then and will continue to do so until they address their problem. This is not to say that an effective passage at one point in life will ensure no crises later. Such crises are an inherent part of life as well as an invitation to further growth. Nevertheless, an early experience of an effective passage can help ward off destructive behavior in response to those later crises because it provides a model of a successful journey.

Former Benchmarks of Maturity

Half a century ago typical benchmarks for young people moving into adulthood included the following: settling into a life work, getting married, creating a home, producing a child, and, for males, going through the military—not necessarily in that order. This, however, is no longer the case. Social and economic circumstances have changed the playing field of life.

A career or "life's work" today takes more preparation and doesn't last a lifetime. Eighteen-year-olds now can expect job and career changes an average of seven times during their lives. Rising housing costs make it harder than ever for young people to afford a home, renting or buying, especially when work is unstable. And marriage and children are being delayed indefinitely.

Or, on the other hand, children are conceiving children without maturity, marriage, work or income to support them. Marriage, above all, once marked arrival at adulthood, but as young adults emerge from childhoods marked by marital unhappiness and single-parent relationships, it's not surprising many are marriage-shy.

Even if these life-events continued to be benchmarks, they would not in themselves guarantee maturity. Any one of them could, on the contrary, be an impediment to maturity. Many mid-aged people know women whose early marriage arrested their intellectual and emotional development, or men who settled too soon into unsuitable life-work only because it seemed to offer security to raise a family.

So look what happens in a society where, on the one hand, all maturity markers disappear: Marriage is delayed or rejected altogether, and sexual expression is no longer identified with such commitment. Young people lack a sense of direction and can't decide what to do with their lives. Establishing a home holds less appeal than going back home to mom and pop. Producing a child is considered a mistake by some in the middle class or a strain on one's freedom, or for under-class teenagers the only thing that symbolizes maturity.

On the other hand, look what happens in a society where the maturity markers have become so materialistic that the three C's become the defining characteristics of adults: the career, condo, and car—and we might add a fourth, the condom.

Postponed Adulthood

Bereft of a culturally-inspired wisdom and empowerment, postponed adulthood among middle-class college graduates[8] often includes these frames of mind:

- in respect to employment, a sense of entitlement and little patience for "paying your dues" at entry-level positions;

- in respect to life style, an anticipation of comfort equal to that earned by mom and dad, and low tolerance for the frugality which life on one's own may demand;

- in respect to responsibility to the world at large, little or no sense of connection to a community beyond one's immediate family and age peers.

Such conditions come out of an egocentric position, relentlessly imprinted by our late 20th century consumer-culture. They lead to two threats: emotional dependence or emotional isolation.

The "forgotten half,"[9] the youngsters who do not go to college, often have their own barriers to adulthood, which may or may not differ from their college-bound peers: materialistic aspirations in conflict with economic deprivation, inadequate parenting and job training, the tyranny of peer harassment, and lack of emotional and spiritual guidance. Hence the multiplication of negative rites of passage, which may include initiation into the local gang or producing a baby, to prove one's "manhood" or "womanhood."[10]

Obviously, more relevant criteria than those promoted by a consumer society could help define maturity. American kids today postpone adulthood because many don't know *how* to grow up. They don't know what it means to be an adult, and they're not getting much help from their elders.

Such wisdom doesn't magically appear at a certain age. Chronological age does not ensure emotional maturity. Growing up demands the transformation of relationships: with parents, with peers, with fellow workers, and with the community at large. The kind of transformation required for adulthood requires the capacity to re-frame[11] one's personal sense of reality.

Framing Reality

A photo exhibit of the work of Alfred Stieglitz[12] graphically demonstrates the effect of framing on perceived meaning. Stieglitz took photo images and cropped them in various ways. The variety of frames—long-shot, close-up, vertical, horizontal—for a single image each invites a different interpretation.

We too frame our experiences, usually unconsciously. In childhood, our frames are tight-in close-ups, very egocentric. If we mature and recognize our connections with ever larger communities, we admit more long-shots into our mental galleries. Each new stage of life challenges us to shift our frame of reference, and each new frame challenges and changes our perception of reality.[13] Somehow we need to become aware of the power of this cinema of the mind. We are only beginning to recognize the implications.

So where do we get these frames of reference? They come from the stories our culture feeds us: stories as essential to the feeding of the psyche as food is to the feeding of the body. The challenge to a culture promoting gossip-filled talk shows and nightly sit-coms to feed story-hungry minds is analogous to promoting light and crispy potato chips and sugar-coated cereal to feed protein-hungry bodies. In both cases severe malnutrition results.

Traditional cultures have provided the stories to frame personal experiences and give insight. Religion was the major provider of stories for a good part of human existence: the stories of the gods and goddesses, the mythical heroes, the Biblical prophets, and the saints. The ancient Greeks recognized the responsibility of the whole community to inspire its youth and provide patterns for behavior through the stories of its heroes.[14] By default, if not by deliberate intent, that role is being taken over today by the advertising and entertainment industries. A sex-symbol like Madonna, rap lyrics, or even the marketing success of a star athlete like Michael Jordan, become the models that contemporary adolescents use to weave their life stories.[15]

Kate, a musician, volunteered time with her son's second grade class during First Communion preparation to teach them several songs for their special Mass. One of the songs was "Kneeling Madonna, fondly we hold thee . . . " In order to make sure the children understood the words they were singing, she asked if they knew who the Madonna was, and all hands shot up. Yet not one (even her own son) identified her as Jesus' mother; all cited the blonde singer. Secular images have swallowed up religious sensibility, even in a Roman Catholic school.

Growing up. Coming to maturity involves learning to "frame" life in healthy, joyful, meaningful ways so one can live with purpose and creativity. People who never grow up are unable to frame their lives at all, and thus see no joy or purpose; or they frame their lives on transient, superficial, and unrealistic values that can't sustain them through difficult times.

A public examination of conscience is going on over the way American culture frames success for young African-American men. It has to do with balance. How many young men in the inner-city sacrifice everything—academics, personal relationships, job skills—for the sake of basketball?[16]

The question is, then, what are these frames? Simply another word for the metaphors—the scripts or myths—we carry in our heads and live out in our lives.[17] From where do these frames or scripts come? Possibly from role models we admire and emulate; but more likely from peers who pressure and push. Possibly from great literature and art; but more likely from soaps and tabloids. Possibly from religious ideals, which stir the spirit; but more likely from advertising that stirs the desires.

Jungian psychologists say that myths come out of the collective unconscious—a kind of shared repository of archetypal human experiences—polluted though they be by present-day culture.[18] Traditional rites taught young initiates to filter their experiences through tribal myths to bring attitudes and behavior into harmony with those of the community at large.[19]

Our myths (or scripts or frames) become the metaphorical spectacles through which we view our lives and hence the filter through which we interpret our experiences. A life viewed through the lens of the soaps and the tabloids is going to have a significantly different quality than one viewed through the lens of a Tolstoy story, a Dickens' novel, or the parables of Jesus. We unconsciously strengthen or construct our myths—our stories—as we go about our lives taking in the multiple messages which continually bombard us.[20]

A major problem in contemporary America is the general lack of skill in filtering the messages and interpreting our experiences. We have lost the way to find or give meaning to what is happening to us. As a result, most of us are suffering from severe psychological indigestion: too many stimuli without a mechanism for filtering, organizing, and digesting the intake.

Dyspeptic psyches are producing unhealthy scripts. We are a people in search of meaning.[21] Yet what we clutch hold of are frenetic images from TV commercials, mixed with soap opera updates and tabloid tales, leaving us fragmented actors bereft of a worthy drama.

This is a problem, to put it mildly, because without some connecting web of understanding, our lives—that is, our own personal dramas—become ". . .just one damn thing after another." So, what do we do about it? There may be some clues to healthier scripts—which is what adulthood is all about—in contemporary thinking.

Challenges of Adulthood

Dealing with Crisis. What is evident to those who study life passages is that each journey from one stage of life to the next is set in motion by a life crisis that cannot be avoided.[22] It may be physical (such as birth, puberty, pregnancy, illness, death), or it may be psychological (such as separation or loss, confrontation with personal limitations, dealing with painful moral choices, or making a sacrifice for a higher value).

For Anne Frank, the 13-year-old Jewish girl living in Holland in 1942, the crisis was going into hiding with her family during the Holocaust. For Nathan McCall, the 19-year-old African American living in Portsmouth, Virginia, in 1975, it was going to prison for armed robbery.[23] The crisis for each of them set in motion their rite of passage. Both crises were extreme, but their very extremity helps highlight the process for us.

Anne's and Nathan's experiences are examples of how an inescapable life crisis—depending on how one handles it—has the power to engender growth. Several factors make this possible:

(1) a secure sense of identity, or ego strength, because this can expand one's ability to interact with others and yet maintain personal stability;

Anne Frank and Nathan McCall offer interesting contrast in this regard. For both, deep social prejudice caused their crisis. In the face of that, both reflected on their sense of identity.

Anne initially had a stronger sense of self for several reasons: She had a close bond with her father; she had a firm sense of her religious and ethnic identity; and she had the ability to recognize and articulate her strengths and weaknesses. When the crisis came, she could deal with it from a strong position and grow in her ability to interact with her fellow "prisoners" in a positive way.

Nathan, on the other hand, at the time of his arrest had no satisfying bond with an elder; his sense of religious and racial identity was wounded and needed healing; his self-criticisms were harsh in the heat of crisis, but he had yet to learn how to use them to re-create a positive sense of self.

(2) a personal set of beliefs, because they provide a sense of direction and a practical guide to behavior, especially in response to life-tasks;

Anne derived great strength from spiritual reflection and prayer. Nathan learned during his time in jail to seek strength from a source beyond himself. He gradually developed his skills—through reading, writing, and reflection—for getting in touch with a higher power.

(3) the ability to symbolize, because it allows the individual to escape the immediate, the personal, and the egocentric, and to move toward an identity with "greatness of Spirit," whether that takes the form of a religious leader—the father Abraham, the Buddha, Jesus Christ or the Virgin Mary, the prophet Mohammed—or the form of the highest of human ideals. To the extent that one moves beyond the realm of petty concerns and toward the realm of spiritual concerns, one expands the capacity for higher level thought and behavior.

Both Anne and Nathan were highly imaginative and dealt creatively with the symbolic realm. Anne's life was swept into a national tragedy with world-wide implications. She was stretched to the limit in coming to terms with life and death, with good and evil. Nathan, on the other hand, was initially trapped in his own small drama, digging himself further and further into trouble in his desperate attempts to save himself. He realized his life has spun out of control.

But two things happened in jail to set in motion his journey toward higher understanding: He learned to value his own racial identity and to acknowledge it as good. He also learned symbolic thinking skills from playing chess with an older prisoner who became his mentor. He discovered that choices have consequences and that he could control the consequences by making thoughtful choices.

These factors—the sense of identity, a personal set of beliefs, and the ability to symbolize—were traditionally built into the rite-of-passage experience and into the religious and educational systems that went with it. But lacking an effective rite of passage in the traditional sense, a secure family structure, a cohesive religious community, or an excellent school can help develop these qualities.

Anne Frank seemed to have had all three in her early life. Nathan's negative self-images so trapped him that he wasn't able even to take advantage of his middle-class suburban life as a youngster. His own grandmother passed along notions about "white folks' superiority." Violent discipline was his model for handling situations. Humiliating treatment of his stepfather by white employers and of himself by white classmates built up in him an anger that was to explode in destructive behavior.

Our national community must find ways to heal generations of wounded young people like Nathan if we are to move out of our cultural adolescence into social maturity.

Satisfying Needs. In addition to a life crisis, another challenge of adulthood is the ability to satisfy physical, psychological, and spiritual needs in healthy ways. Abraham Maslow's hierarchy of needs is relevant to a discussion of growth because he brought to public attention the idea that individuals grow by satisfying physiological and safety needs before they can move on to the satisfaction of higher psychological and spiritual needs.[24] If the lower order needs have been adequately satisfied at some point in life, an individual can later be deprived of food, shelter, and safety and still move into higher order needs and their satisfaction.

Although Maslow did not deal with rites of passage, it is noteworthy that traditional rites of initiation into adulthood challenge the entire range of physical and psychological needs identified in his theory: the needs for food, shelter, safety, for a sense of belonging and love, for competence and achievement. The paradox is that the crisis engendered by the true rite of passage involves a painful challenge to these needs: physically—through fasting, hardships, threats to a personal sense of safety and security; and psychologically—through separation from home and loved ones, removal of status, tests of competence. At the same time that the lower physical and psychological needs are being challenged, ways open up to fulfill the higher spiritual needs—transcending one's personal concerns, working for the good of others, discovering a power that lies beyond the self.

In contemporary America where emphasis on comfort and sensuality has reached hedonistic levels for many, there is widespread refusal to challenge one's often unbridled satisfaction of physical needs. One's comfort level has become the most common criterion for choices and decisions. How often do we hear the expression, "I'm not comfortable with that"?

On the other hand, if youngsters have not had adequate satisfaction of physical needs such as nutritious food, appropriate clothing, and adequate safety; and psychological needs such as a sense of belonging and love, competence and respect; then it's almost impossible for them to develop their capacity for satisfying their higher spiritual needs unless some extraordinary intervention comes into their lives. The cry of inner-city youth, for instance, for respect, and the volatile nature of "disrespect" or "dissing," is a clear reminder of the importance of this psychological need. It will not be ignored.

Taking on New Roles. In addition to dealing with crises and satisfying needs, we come to the third challenge of adulthood. Studies demonstrate that when young people find themselves in situations where they are challenged by tasks that lift them out of their egocentric perspective, they can rise to meet the challenge and grow in the process. A key factor in this kind of growth is the importance of taking on a new role.[25]

The theater metaphor works well here. Similar to the actor who takes on a dramatic role, transforming his perspective and behavior to fit that role; so a former gang member can take on the role of caring for a youngster in a wheel chair, or a suburban cheerleader can go into the wilderness and learn to fight forest fires.

In their new roles, he and she begin to see themselves as people who can share their sensitivity and strength by serving a need beyond their immediate world, In the process, they learn of their own unique worth to the human community. Hence, the importance of providing roles that uplift (that of "big brother" or conservation corps member) rather than demean (juvenile delinquent or "feather-brain").

The developmental psychologist Erik Erikson suggests the major challenge of adolescence is consolidation of a stable identity in the face of all that would fragment: advertising, peer pressure, family problems, and so on.[26] For both Anne Frank and Nathan McCall, taking on a new role triggered the evolution of their new identities. Anne, first unconsciously, later deliberately, took on the role of documentarian of her family's two years in hiding from the Nazis. Nathan volunteered to become jail librarian early in his term.

These freely chosen roles triggered their personal journeys in ways neither could have predicted. In addition, their persistent reflection and writing in their journals profoundly shaped the development of their identity in the face of severe crisis.

Restructuring Psychic Energy. Such roles can restructure one's inner energy, a fourth challenge of adulthood. One becomes mature precisely by focusing energy, which, in the juvenile state, has been scattered and capricious, and directing it toward appropriate behavior.[27] Therefore, good habit formation at a young age is critical because it makes appropriate behavior more spontaneous and less exhausting.[28] Of course, what is appropriate is a standard set by one's culture. Traditional expectations were imprinted on the young by rites of passage and religion. Contemporary expectations are imprinted by parents (where they are active and effective), the classroom (often not very successfully), by rap, television, and films, and by hanging out at the malls and on the streets with peers.

Depending on rap, television and films to imprint cultural expectations and restructure energy is not wise, as studies of the impact of their violence can attest.[29] The urge to imitate became particularly apparent when a scene from the Disney film "The Program" stimulated three teenagers, within days after viewing the film, to lie down on a highway in the path of oncoming vehicles to prove their toughness. One was killed; two were critically injured. The distributor subsequently pulled the film from the theaters and removed that scene.[30]

Getting the Kids to Grow Up

So, how do we get the kids to grow up in a healthy way? The challenges of adulthood and the patterns suggested by myths, rites of passage and religious rituals give us suggestions. Social and personal experiences such as apprenticeships and internships, Scouting[31] and church camps, the civil rights movement, Outward Bound,[32] and the military, provide paths to adulthood.[33] Each of these options has valuable elements. Each can be examined against a set of criteria for all effective rites of passage.[34]

One choice in particular, however, seems especially effective in accomplishing the intellectual, psychological, and spiritual tasks which face young people at this critical juncture in life: some form of intensive service experience, what has come to be known as "youth service." Moreover, some of the most effective "youth service" has been going on for decades. Furthermore, these service experiences share a basic pattern found in tribal and religious rites, even in the negative rites described in the popular media.

Patterns of Experience. Let's examine this pattern in the face of what *should* happen on the journey to adulthood and see if we can find healthier ways to grow up in today's world. Consider the following:

• Importance of risk.

In each of these activities is the need to prove manhood or womanhood. Examples from contemporary life include tracking, chicken, riding the tops of elevators, and teenage pregnancy. Each of these behaviors involves taking a chance, stepping out "on the tightrope." Each represents "proof" of courage, strength, and timing. But a healthier form of "walking a tightrope," and doing it literally, is the high ropes course that is now an important part of a number of contemporary youth experiences. Another form of risk-taking is reading from the Torah in Hebrew before several hundred people. In national service settings young people are taking on the challenge of working elbow to elbow with others who grew up in different racial, ethnic, and religious backgrounds. To reach across barriers such as these is emotionally risky business.

- Importance of separation.

Every May the local newspapers tout the spring prom as a rite of passage; the high school students separate themselves from the classroom, the streets, and shopping mall to enter the elegant world of the hotel ballroom. All of this is, of course, a very superficial analogy to a true rite of passage, but one thing is right: the element of separation. In a tribal world, the young people are removed from their homes and taken to the place of transformation, whether it is into the forest for the boys or into the menstrual hut for the girls.

When the contemporary youngster goes off to join a conservation corps in a national park or to become a member of an urban corps in an inner city, the change of setting brings with it less chance of carrying with one the old role—the role of son or daughter of so-and-so, or student in such-and-such high school. It signals the beginning of a new life where there is less chance of being treated as what one was before and more chance of being treated as what one is now.

Such a change also gives more opportunity for expanding one's mental as well as geographical horizon. The young person, having separated from home base, is more likely to return home transformed and to be treated as such.

- Importance of a role shift.

Initiation into gangs or induction into fraternities brings with the membership new roles. The role gives a youth the opportunity to put on a new set of attitudes and behavior much like an actor dons a costume. Often in contemporary culture the new role brings with it a uniform. It might be a waiter's outfit for the new job, or it may be the red jacket and khaki pants of City Year in Boston or the deep green of a conservation corps member in a western state park. The uniform of the armed services and the role shift that it represents has been a traditional "maturity marker" in our culture. (Whether warranted or not is another matter.) Full-time service, however, demands a more complete role-shift than part-time service, giving the former an advantage over the latter.

- Importance of new responsibilities.

Religious rites bring to the young person's awareness certain obligations that he or she now has as an "adult" member of the community. These obligations involve observing the rules and laws of the religion, often following certain dietary prescriptions, and observing a spiritual discipline.

These responsibilities may decline as the years go by, but within a tribal culture the rite of passage into adulthood is irrevocable: The responsibilities of maturity are now the expected behavior. Teenage mothers also take on new responsibilities, as inappropriate as they may be. It is a mark of achievement to have produced a baby, and a high proportion of unwed mothers refuse to give up their infants for adoption. Peace Corps volunteers soon discover in their new setting that they not only have the new responsibilities of their assigned task but also the responsibilities that go with being a representative of the United States of America. This is quite an awakening to the youth who has up to that point been aware only of his or her personal, private life.

- Importance of new relationships.

Within the tribal culture the bonding of age cohorts among the young men is an essential part of their rite of passage experience. The bonding of the young women is more likely to come among those who share the same domestic tasks or even the same husband. In contemporary culture the bondings of gang members, of fraternities and of sororities share many similarities. They all go through initiation ordeals; they commit themselves to absolute loyalty to the group, and their relationships with each other take on the feel of a family. The relationships, too, among youth corps members take on a highly committed, loyal, and strong bond. To work together on a task that enables young people to transcend racial, ethnic, social, and religious barriers creates a powerful covenant indeed.

- Importance of empowerment.

Native Americans of the North American plains structured the empowerment of their young men through the vision quest. They encouraged their sons to seek personal power by solitude and fasting, often going to "the breaking point of physical suffering in the hope of entering into communication with the sacred world."[35]

In contemporary American culture possession of a gun is a symbol of empowerment for today's youth. In contrast with such a violent expression of power, a program in East Harlem has been working for over two decades to train youth to empower themselves through leadership development.[36] It is now evident that young people possess authentic power only when they share decision-making roles with their adult leaders. Youth corps leaders around the country, inspired by the East Harlem program, are building empowerment into the corps experience. Inherent in youth service philosophy is the recognition of young people's intelligence and capacity to make positive choices.

- Importance of new knowledge.

For the most part tribal rites of passage were an investment in tribal identity and a test of survival skills by undergoing a survival situation. As such, there was an inherent motive to hone these skills to the maximum. Young people in American culture often derive their identity from the neighborhood, the gang, or the professional sports team logo emblazoned across their backs. On the other hand, members of youth service corps develop skills in ecology and social service, in math and English for GED completion where needed, in conflict resolution, and, above all, in reflection.

Corps leaders recognize that service activities, while good in themselves, are not enough to contribute to the development of the youth involved. They need something more—the capacity for reflection.[37] Only through reflection can the most important knowledge of all be obtained, the knowledge of one's self in the context of a community. This is essential to the journey from me to we.

- Importance of community recognition.

To be seen by one's community as having achieved a new status validates the new self-image; it is a form of "confirmation."[38] Tribal youth and their communities recognize that the rite of passage changes them forever; there is no going back to childhood. In the contemporary world, the debutante experience is a way of "introducing" the young woman to society—a way of gaining community recognition—and is often referred to as a rite of passage. High school and college graduations are a public recognition of academic achievements of a group of young people. Youth service programs also have recognized the value of a community recognition—a "graduation" if you will—with a certificate to mark the occasion.

Implications

The Hero's Journey. The heroic impulse is part of our urge to perform our manhood and womanhood, to act it out in ways that draw the spotlight and elicit attention and approval, even if only momentarily. The young men and women on the street often are performing their "manhood" and "womanhood" destructively because they don't see other more appropriate ways to act it out. Each generation will create its own performance; but the elders must teach them how to do it right.

"Doing it right" is all about awakening a sense of responsibility. Dr. Viktor Frankl, who drew attention to the "search for meaning" in emotional and spiritual health, made a significant discovery in this regard.[39] As a young doctor in Austria before World War II, he identified what he called "unemployment neurosis." Thousands of young people who were jobless felt useless. For them, being useless meant having a meaningless life.

He further discovered that feeling empty and meaningless leads to what he called an "existential vacuum," a dangerous condition, the characteristics of that syndrome being depression, aggression, and addiction. He learned, however, that when he was successful in persuading his clients to volunteer—to devote some of their free time to unpaid but meaningful activity—their depression disappeared in spite of their unchanged economic situation.

Frankl put it this way: "The truth is that man does not live by welfare alone."[40]   Lest we view this as an

74

invitation to slash job programs, we must recognize that however therapeutic volunteering is on an individual level, mass unemployment (and the resulting sense of meaninglessness) is pernicious on a cultural level—as history bore out.

Still, given a relatively healthy economy, a path that seems especially effective in accomplishing the intellectual, psychological, and spiritual challenges that face youth in their late teens and early 20s is some form of intensive service experience.

The name it goes under can be problematic. "Community service" has taken on a negative connotation by association with the penal system and the term corrupted because of make-work and poor monitoring.[41] "National service" seems to limit the idea to federal government-supported programs. "Volunteer work" often conveys the image of Lady Bountiful and one-way do-goodism.[42] "Youth service" implies that only youth can participate. Nevertheless, because this book focuses on youth, I will use the term "youth service."

In spite of the recent upsurge of interest in youth service, it is important to realize that some of the most effective programs have been going on for decades. Thousands upon thousands of young people have participated. In the case of the old Civilian Conservation Corps (CCC), millions took part. What might those who undertook the service challenge during those years contribute to the public discussion today?

* * *

Part II. The Heroic Journey

Touchstones on the Path to Maturity

T he ancients discovered they could test the quality of gold by looking at the streak it left when rubbed against a type of dark stone. The stones came to be called touchstones. Over time the word touchstone came to stand for any criterion of quality or genuineness.

So, then, what are the life-experience touchstones on the road to maturity? What standards should we look for when thinking about events that will help our young people grow up?

The mythical path of "the hero" offers clues. It follows the same pattern as the traditional rites of passage: separation, initiation, incorporation. Joseph Campbell, the comparative mythologist, in his work *The Hero With a Thousand Faces*,[1] was the first to suggest this parallel between the "hero's journey"—an underlying pattern he found in mythology of all cultures—and tribal rites of passage. Both share the separation from home and all that is familiar, the initiation into the world between what was and what is to come—where one undertakes a task and undergoes a transformation—and the return (incorporation) to the community as a new individual. Since ancient times these patterns of experience have been significant— although not necessarily universal—touchstones of growing up.

In using the parallel which Campbell points out, however, I have chosen to shift the focus from the hero to the journey. Rather than using the term "hero's journey," I choose to call the coming-of-age experiences the "heroic journey" and focus on the process rather than the protagonist. The "hero's journey" seems to convey a kind of solitary individualistic quest for self-glory;[2] whereas the "heroic journey" conveys a process that demands a gift of self for a purpose beyond the self. By its very nature, achieving adulthood demands some sort of heroic sacrifice in order to expand the human capacity for taking on the attitudes and behavior appropriate for maturity.

With Campbell's work as background, I have identified seven "touchstones" embedded in the "heroic journey." They provide a vocabulary for talking about and assessing this transition in life.[3] Each touchstone reveals the "gold" to be found in the experience: that is, the qualities within the challenge for bringing about psychological, social, and spiritual transformation. The touchstones are the following:

- the call,
- departure,
- encounter with the guardian spirit,
- taking on the task,
- battle with the beast,
- victory, and
- the return.

A society must identify the destination as well as the path to maturity. How does one know when he or she has arrived? Anthropologist David Gilmore provides a succinct description of the critical threshold: "the point at which the boy produces more than he consumes and gives more than he takes."[4] This definition holds every bit as true for the young woman as for the young man.

Hence my thesis: If the challenge of moving into adulthood is a transformation from emphasis on taking to that on giving, then an intensive service experience coupled with reflection can trigger that transformation.

The following chapters are based on four dozen interviews with men and women who have participated in a non-military service experience in their late teens and early 20s. (Two of them include their military experience in addition to their non-military service.) All of their stories bear striking resemblance to the heroic journey.

Remember, as discussed in Chapter One, a rite of passage is not some kind of technique that magically transforms an adolescent into an adult. It is, rather, a community-supported experience which by its nature forces young people symbolically to die to the stage of life they have outgrown and to be reborn to a new more appropriate stage. With at least a minimal understanding of what is happening comes the transformation.

Chapter Four

Separation:
"It's hard to let go."

The Call: *"Let's get a little excitement outta life."*

Challenge: to develop the ability to listen
to the inner voice
and to have the faith to follow it.

Jim is an Illinois High School Coaches' Hall of Fame figure three times over: football, basketball, and baseball. A coach for close to 50 years, Jim remembers his "call" to the Civilian Conservation Corps:

> In western Minnesota in those days—that was 1936, the
> dust-bowl days—there was absolutely nothing there.
> You could see nothing but hopelessness. The dust was
> blowing like crazy. It was April. One day it was pitch

dark, and I told my mother, "Now I'm going to leave . . .
go some place . . . I'm just going to go."

At that time they were recruiting for the CCCs. I was
17, a senior in high school. I had not graduated yet. I
had two months left to go. So I went and asked the
principal of the school if I could graduate if I went and
joined the CCCs. He said I could. So another fellow and
I went to Tunerville, Minn., a one-car stop on the local
rail.

There is something so enticing about the call to
adventure that when a young person hears it, it's almost
impossible to ignore. To refuse the call is to quench some
vital energy. And yet to accept a call which is destructive,
because the youth must break out of a life that has become
too small, causes both personal and community crisis.
Parents and community elders should be asking: What kinds
of "calls" are enticing our youngsters? what kinds of
responses are young people making?

In tribal cultures the call of the young woman was
physiological: Her first menstruation was the signal that her
status within the community had changed forever. The call
of the young man was not so specific. His father, along with
the elders of the village, recognized when it was time for
him to leave the world of the mother and to respond to the
world of the men.

From the time of pre-history the call of the warrior
has framed the development of the young male in just about
every culture known to man. Until some other image of
manhood is held before our youth, the call to war will
continue to define masculinity. William James recognized
the power of war to focus youthful energy and attention,
and recommended a "moral equivalent of war."[1] What can
spark the energy and focus the attention of young men the
way facing an enemy can? Research presently argues that

engaging in challenging service projects that demand physical and moral strength and perseverance.[2]

So "the call" repeats itself from one generation to the next in the lives of young people. A challenge is put forth, either by some external force—such as drought and depression did for Jim—or a draft notice, admission to college or a new job; or by some internal force, such as a longing to prove one's strength or courage, to travel, to be helpful, or to master a particular skill. By its nature, such a call pulls young people out of what they were, toward what they can become.

For Doris, in nursing school in 1941, the call came the day after Pearl Harbor:

> The university hospital where I was in training had been one of the reserve hospitals. Pearl Harbor was bombed on a Sunday. By Monday all the doctors and nurses were coming to work in their green uniforms. I thought, Oh, this looks so dramatic and so exciting—I want to be in the Army. By 1943, when I was a senior, I signed up with the Red Cross, which did much of the recruiting for military nurses in those days.

For Loretta, now a Jungian analyst in private practice, the call came just after World War II. She recalls:

> I had graduated from college and had one year of [internship] experience with [psychiatrist] Bruno Bettelheim when I applied to the American Friends Service Committee Relief Program. They had relief workers in Germany with the British Quakers. The British Quakers in the British zone of occupation of Germany were allowed to have non-military personnel. The American zone did not allow that. So I was one of the 20 Americans sent to work with the British Quakers.

83

I went in 1947, keenly aware of my eagerness to be of
service.

Some young people of the generation of the 1950s
responded to the challenge of Harry Truman, put forth in his
Inaugural Address of 1949, in what came to be known as
the Point Four Program. Others, like Ed, were caught
between the desire for civilian service and the call to military
service. Ed recalls:

> As soon as I graduated in 1950 I went to England to
> work with a student exchange program called
> International Association for the Exchange of Students
> for Technical Experience. My job was with the Dunlop
> Rubber Company in Birmingham. About two days after
> I arrived in England the Korean War broke out. About a
> month later I got my draft notice.
>
> I wrote to Truman saying that I thought I could better
> serve my country and my fellow man by going to Africa
> than as a draftee. I got a letter back from the Selective
> Service saying that was not an option. So I decided to
> compare the two forms of service: the military and, if I
> survived, service in a civilian capacity.
>
> In the Army I was assigned to the Signal Corps. I did
> my basic training at Fort Dix, N.J. It was the standard
> 14 weeks or so. Most of the people were sent over to
> Korea, but since I had a university degree in physics,
> they sent me to Fort Monmouth, N.J. I was there for a
> year. Then they needed somebody with the same
> background at the White Sands Proving Ground in New
> Mexico. So I was sent there for about seven months. I
> finished up my service out in New Mexico and was
> discharged from the base there at El Paso.
>
> I went to Nigeria in the summer of '53, not quite 25
> years old. The position came through the International

Development Placement Association (IDPA). The
organization only lasted for two or three years and then
ran out of money. They were set up to find jobs in
developing countries. Job application #1 was for a
science teacher in Molusi College in Ijebu Igbo, Nigeria.
That's the one I ended up filling.

For many college graduates of the 1960s the image
of a young President asking them, "Think not of what your
country can do for you. Think of what you can do for your
country," rang in their ears as they signed up for Peace
Corps and Volunteers in Service to America (VISTA). Ben,
now a director of a private secondary school, remembers
when Kennedy gave his speech at the University of
Michigan:

> The next day my twin brother and I both
> independently—we were at different universities—
> picked up the *New York Times* and reached for the
> phone. We spent the morning trying to get in touch with
> each other and say, "This is it. This is what we want.
> This is what we've been waiting for."

Carol, the director of a national association in
Washington, D.C., joined VISTA in 1970 and worked with
the Native Americans in Montana. She remembers her call:

> I heard about the Peace Corps from President Kennedy
> back in the early '60s when the program was created.
> And then VISTA came along. I think all of us were
> inspired by that President at the time. There was a sense
> of duty. Although I was still in college, I decided that
> was something I was definitely going to do. And so I
> did.

For Erika, now a counselor in an urban shelter for
women, the call was her desire for adventure, to go to

someplace far away from her Iowa farm life. Her church offered her several options. As a senior at Goshen College (Mennonite) in the late '80s, she participated in the cultural experience expected of all the students: living, learning, and doing service in another country—a cultural exchange. She chose Costa Rica to take advantage of her new skills in Spanish:

> I was drawn to adventure . . . always. In our small town my friend and I used to joke about how we were going to go to some exotic place . . . like England—you know, experience the world—'cause this was such a small place. . . . When I first became aware of this desire, I was thinking more of poor people in far-away places that were very distant from me. Because I have so much, I thought I needed to leave here. Everyone has so much around where I live. . . . But that's not necessarily true. I realize that now. But then, it looked like I needed to go overseas or far away to do the kind of service I had in my mind.

Deliah, now a teacher with her husband in Denver, remembers why they chose to go to Belize with the Jesuit International Volunteers (JIV) in 1989:

> We were both journalism/advertising majors. It took us four years in college to figure out that's not what we wanted to do. We talked a lot about service work and really the only thing we knew of was the Peace Corps because that's well-publicized. But we were looking into ideas other than the Peace Corps because we wanted it to have a spiritual bent. That was really important to us. And we wanted to find a program that would take us soon after we were married. After looking into a number of options, we decided on the JIV.

Bill, who graduated from high school in 1990, remembers why he joined City Year at that point:

I was just burnt out. I mean I had gone to a pretty intensive intellectual high school. I had a good academic career, but I needed a break to give me a little leeway before college. I didn't really know what I wanted to do for that year. My dad came up with news articles about new programs and new ideas.

Out of all the new ideas, City Year just seemed like the perfect program. I couldn't imagine a better program. Just being in Boston . . . at the time I wanted to go to school there as well. I had never been there. I felt it would be a good way to get a feel for the city as well as continuing the volunteer work I had started in high school.

It also contained the diversity that I find so important. I mean, growing up in an interracial family—I'm the oldest and three of my siblings are adopted—diversity is a pretty important thing to me. And City Year seemed to be one of the few organizations that really sought to provide that. In fact, after me, two of my brothers did City Year too. But my peers didn't think much of the idea. It was an understood thing, coming out of my high school, you just went directly to college. No ifs, ands, or buts about it. But I just knew that wasn't the route I wanted to go.

Ruth, a single mother of two daughters, was watching her life fall apart in spite of her recent degree in journalism. She couldn't get adequate work to support herself and her two daughters, so she ended up in a homeless shelter. She recalls:

This was a bitter pill to swallow. I wanted to work. I constantly asked my caseworker, "Do you offer employment programs?" She said, "I didn't sign you up for the program because you have a degree." I said,

"Well, that may be true, but I don't have a job. I need a
job if I'm going to get off welfare." It was a handicap if
you had anything above a high school diploma. They
felt that you were trying to abuse the system.

A friend of mine who worked at the homeless shelter
asked if I knew about VISTA. I didn't. But the shelter
had an opening for a VISTA. Discovering this would be
a real job, I filled out the application and was honest
about all the problems I was facing. Two days later I got
a call for an interview.

Ruth little realized, when she was selected for the
position, the journey that would open up to her.

While it is always possible to refuse or ignore such
calls, the more probable reaction is to respond. However, if
we look at the media for today's choices of "rites of
passage," we discover that too often the response is
frivolous or downright destructive. A society must provide
healthy opportunities. Some of the options presented in the
mass media range from getting nose or nipple rings to
hanging out on the mall to "getting blasted" on the beach
during spring break. Young people want proof of their
independence, their uniqueness, their worth, their courage,
their achievement. The community has a responsibility to
help young people to grow up precisely by providing the
kinds of challenges that are worthy of their youthful energy
and attention. To turn this stage of life into a marketing
cohort is a fact of American economic life, but to leave it
there is to trivialize it.

The Departure: *"I'm Outta Here."*

Challenge: to develop the capacity to make the
necessary sacrifice(s) to respond to the call
and thereby to become independent.

Once the reality of separation sets in, the recognition
of the sacrifices entailed in this adventure takes hold
of the young seeker. Every adventure demands its
price. Paying the price is often a real shock. Jim remembers
as he set off in 1936 for the CCC:

> It was really quite a jolt for me. I had lived away from
> home during the past several summers. but this was
> going to be forever. I enlisted in Morris, Minn., and they
> took us up to Fort Snelling. Gave us our shots. It was
> very depressing because you were in the dark Army
> barrack, and you could watch what was left of the U.S.
> Army. The fellows were throwing manure and caring for
> the mules, and that was about it.

> Then I was taken from there up to Duluth. We got on
> Army convoys and went to Grand Marais, Minn. and
> then back in the woods some 60 miles. It was a rough,
> rough ride [quivering voice]. We got up there, and they
> had built barracks for probably 175 young fellows, who
> were all in the same condition I was. There was nothing
> for them to do at home. Their parents needed the money,
> 'cause remember $25 a month went home, and the guys
> in camp got $5. We were there for six months. Sixty
> miles from town and there was no way we were going to
> get to town. Nobody was going to hike that 60 miles
> down the Gunflint Trail. So that was the start.

Separation from home for Ed, who spent two years in the Army and then went to Africa in 1953, had occurred during high school:

> My father died when I was 14. My mother went back to school. When she got her teaching certificate and a job, she went about twenty miles away. I just had a semester to finish at the high school, so I stayed with a family in the city there.

The price is often paid by the parents as well as the young volunteer. Julie, a former Jesuit Volunteer Corps member (1989-90), recalls her parents' reaction to her decision to go to Alaska with the JVC for a year:

> My parents were disappointed that I wasn't coming home. They lived in Tennessee. That's where I grew up. I had been in college in New Orleans. They were really expecting me to move back and to be at home and be with them. I am number nine out of nine children.
>
> It was in January or February of senior year and I was having a phone conversation with my father. I said I want you to know I'm going to do a volunteer program after graduation. He wasn't angry or anything like that. He just said, "Well, I know a volunteer program you can do. You can come to Central Avenue (which is our address) and you can take care of these two old people." I let them know I wanted to go to Alaska.
>
> My mother said, "Why Alaska? Why can't you do it here in Nashville? Or do it in New Orleans. Do it in someplace you know."
>
> I said, "The point is, I want to go away to some place new, to some place real different." They were disappointed that I wasn't coming back. They weren't angry, but they weren't supportive either. I mean, they

didn't tell me, "Oh, this is great! We're so proud of you." They never said that. But the reaction they started getting from family and friends was, "Oh, that's so great! You must be so proud of her." I think it began to dawn on them . . . and they would relate those stories to me: "Sister Mary Angela told us how proud of you she is!"

None of my brothers and sisters had done anything like that. I know that in a way they took it as me just trying to be a rebel or different, just trying to exert my independence, so I think they just kind of rolled their eyes about that. "Oh, she's just got to go away and be different and do something crazy. This is attention-getting."

I did have an argument with one of my sisters once. This was after my volunteer year. My sister said, "You need to be home now. You've had your fun." She really interpreted my going to Alaska and doing my volunteer year as skirting my responsibilities. "You got to go away and have a fun year in a big house full of young people and play around. Now you've got to grow up and come home and help take care of our parents." Seven of their nine children live in Nashville. They're 69 years old. My father works forty hours a week. They're fine.

Putting Things into Perspective

Every departure, no matter how exhilarating the upcoming adventure, demands its price. In tribal cultures the young man going on his vision quest fasts for days at a time as he searches for the dream that will reveal his place in life. The young woman goes into seclusion outside the village border and is isolated for the time being from the companionship of her peers. So today, the comforts and familiarity of home are given up. Family relationships will be forever altered, the companionship of peers left behind. Some force or power must come to the fore to compel the young person to continue to pursue the adventure into the unknown in spite of the price he or she must pay.

Often in the case of negative rites of passage the force is fear. Fear of being called a coward or being beaten up—as kids are when they resist joining the neighborhood gang; fear of being ostracized from the peer group—as boys are who refuse to respond to the challenge of chicken; fear of being thought odd or strange or weird—as girls are who choose to remain virgins. Other times the force may be a restlessness with life the way it is, a feeling that one has outgrown the old; and the young person feels compelled to experiment with addictive substances or flirt with outrageous perils.

Any one of these forces may lead to a rite of passage, but adult wisdom is essential to steer the young seeker in the right direction. Additional, more positive, forces may include a drive to master certain skills that necessitates leaving home to find the best teachers, or a yen for adventure that demands a new arena for activity.

Bill went into his City Year experience with no preconceived notions. As far as he was concerned, he wasn't losing anything, he was gaining everything. But then he discovered how difficult it was to arrange for his living quarters, and he had to deal with it by himself over the phone from North Carolina where his family was on vacation:

> I got into City Year late. So a lot of people had gotten housing and had worked out the arrangements. It was not easy because it was already into August. City Year provided me with a list of people who were also looking for housing. I was nervous. I mean, over the phone, I was trying to get a feel for what these people were like and whether or not I would want to live with them.

But I discovered four guys had a place in Somerville, right outside of Cambridge. It was cheap rent but a nice location. They were like, if you don't mind bunking with another person, hop in. I was never used to having my own room, so that was not a factor. It was the five of us living together. It turned out to be a great living arrangement. I was lucky.

Don, from Colorado, was studying Latin-American culture at an eastern urban university when he decided that his language skills would be most benefited by spending a semester in South America. Desiring something more than the typical exchange student experience, he discovered The Partnership for Service-Learning which offers study abroad programs at the college level linking community service and academic study. He chose the program in Ecuador and set off in January of 1991 by way of Argentina. He recalls,

> My flight from Buenos Aries to Quito was canceled, so I was delayed by a week. I had sent them a FAX, but apparently it never reached them so no one knew that I was coming in. I landed in Quito and then had to take another flight to my assigned city, Guayaquil, the industrial port on the coast of Ecuador. It doesn't get a lot of press because it's a big ugly city but very tropical. It's the biggest city in Ecuador. I didn't know anything about this city before I went there. All Americans hear about is Quito and the Galapagos Islands.
>
> It was pouring rain when I arrived at the airport. All I had was the phone number of the director of the program. I called. He wasn't home. He was out with the group of Americans on a field trip. His wife answered. She is Ecuadorian but speaks English. By this time I had been practicing my Spanish that short time in Argentina, but, still, over the phone—you're disoriented and you don't know where you are. It's a

foreign country. There is no one there to meet you. I was freaking out. There I was standing in the airport, soaking wet. It was close to midnight. I didn't know if anyone was coming to get me. I wanted to go home. At that point I was thinking, "Get me out of here!" . . . But then you're like, I'm here. I might as well make the most of it.

She told me in broken English, "I'll be there. I'll come pick you up. Don't worry." She did come. But by this time the streets of the city were flooded. There's no drainage system in Guayaquil. I just happened to arrive during monsoon season.

On the way to the home of my host family, she told me they had come to the airport a week ago with a sign saying, "Welcome, Don, to Ecuador." When I didn't get off the plane, no one knew where I was. They had no idea what was going on. My host mother was in tears: "What happened to my American son? He deserted us."

By the time we reached the neighborhood of my host family, we were unable to go to the house because of the amount of water in the streets. So she told me . . . kind of like, "Go down this street." She couldn't leave her car." Your host mother knows you are coming. Take your stuff."

I got out of the car with my luggage on my head and waded through half a foot of dirty, yukky water. I wade down the street, and all I see is this tiny Ecuadorian woman waving hysterically with tears running down her cheeks, probably thinking, "He's finally arrived." I must have been like a vision of a saint or something.

The moment I walked into the house, she gave me a towel and tried to dry me off. I was like her son from the minute I came. She was the most wonderful person.

That incident brought us together real quick. It was an unfortunate experience, but it got me in the mode to put things into perspective. It was a good start. There's a lot more important things than getting wet and being inconvenienced. I started out with a real positive attitude. We laughed about it for the next three months.

Simple Life Style

The modest living stipend provided by the youth corps imposes a simple life style on the volunteers unless a bank account back home or doting parents supplement it. In the case of the religious-based corps, such as the Jesuit, Lutheran, and Mennonite Corps, the expectation is a deliberately-chosen simple life style. Barbara, a Jesuit Volunteer Corps member (1990-92) who spent one year in Boston and a second in Dallas, was concerned about money and the implications of its lack on her life:

> One of my greatest fears was financial. Am I going to be able to survive on my stipend of $85/month? The point of it is the simple life style. You have to live modestly on that $85. We got separate money for food, and that went into a community fund. We didn't have to pay rent or utilities. So really that $85/month was for our personal use. In our community we had two people who were second year volunteers. They were into simple living and believed in that whole idea. I was kind of in between and didn't know quite how I felt about it. I was probably leaning more toward not wanting to live a simple life style. We did talk about it a little bit. Another woman was very honest. She said, "I joined the Jesuit Volunteer Corps because I wanted to help people. I'm not into this simple life style thing."

When I was in Dallas [during my second year], we were
discussing whether or not we were living simply. I don't
think we lived that simple, whereas another housemate
thought we did live simply. I said to him, "How do you
think we're living simply?" He said, "I'm using the
powdered detergent—and that gets caught in my clothes
—rather than a liquid. I enjoy meat and I'm not eating
meat. We don't have meat. And that's a simple life
style."

Whereas, for me, using the powdered soap or not eating
meat wasn't a big deal. I think a lot of it depends on
what sacrifice means to the individual because using the
powdered soap [cheaper] didn't bother me so I didn't
think of it as a sacrifice.

One issue for us in Boston was how high should we
keep the heat. We didn't need to pay for heat but it was
the idea of simple living. We requested a certain amount
of money from our supporting organization for each
month. If our heating bill was higher, then we would
have to go to them.

The kind of foods we would buy was an issue. Not all
the JVC houses are committed to vegetarianism. It's up
to the individual houses to work that out. JVC set before
us reasons behind vegetarianism. They expressed to us
the idea that it takes so much grain to keep a cow alive.
It has to do with resources for the rest of the world.

There was one woman in our house, about half way
through the year she decided she was going to be a strict
vegetarian. She didn't eat anything that had been living:
no chicken, no fish. It turned out that milk bothered her.
I think the lactose got to her. It got to the point where
she couldn't have dairy products, and that had been her
mainstay. I think that she could have done better had
she actually cooked for herself. Instead of eating a real

meal, she ended up eating sweets. I don't think that was a very good diet for her to be on.

As far as the food thing went, it's kind of a tradition among the JVCs to be kind of heavy on the beans and rice. They supplied us with a cookbook. All the foods in it are very cheap foods, how you can get a lot for your money kind of thing, and it has healthy recipes. So I don't know how much instruction we needed, but it might have been helpful to mention it during orientation if you were going to get along without meat then you do need to watch your diet.

Actually there was one thing that they did say: "If you're cold or you're hungry, if you're not meeting your own basic needs, then you can't take care of others." So they definitely didn't want us to starve ourselves.

Erika, in the Mennonite Volunteer Corps (1990-91), describes her situation:

The stipend comes from the supporting agency. It was $600 a month for us. But instead of us seeing the check, it would go straight into a big pool and we would get $30 a month to spend. It [the $600 stipend minus the $30] would pay for rent, food, things like shampoo, necessary kinds of toiletries that we would all share, and a car which we all shared. The program coordinator kind of oversaw the finances.

The Peace Corps had its own way of advocating a simple life style: expecting the volunteers to live at the economic level of the people they served. But sometimes the living stipend would put the volunteer in a different category, as Nate discovered when he went to Bangladesh in 1963:

My subsistence allowance was $80 a month when I was in Bangladesh. That put me at the same salary as my headmaster, and I was making more than my fellow teachers. Of course, the cost of living is cheap, but it meant that I had to live like they did. I couldn't go out and rent my own place and bring in a stereo. We had a dining hall where I ate part of the time, but there was concern over the quality of the food.

One of the big things the Peace Corps is concerned about is that you eat right and that the food be prepared right. In the school hostels they can't always guarantee that the cooks are washing their hands. Dysentery and things like that are endemic. So to keep volunteers healthy, they wanted us to have our own food-preparers, but a lot of times you end up eating in the hostel anyway because if somebody invites you or there's a holiday, you go eat there.

At first you're scared to eat anything when you arrive. Then the pendulum goes the other way and you eat things you shouldn't. You get sick . . . and then you strike a happy medium.

Privacy

Sometimes the price of the adventure is so painful that the only thing that keeps the young pilgrim going is the fear of being the first to give up in the face of the other volunteers. Nate, the Peace Corps alumnus, remembers his traumatic experience:

The hardest thing to get used to was that Bangladesh is a country about the same size as Wisconsin, and at that time Wisconsin had about three million population and Bangladesh had 100 million people. So you'd think, I'll just go down this road and spend some time by myself, but there would be people all over. Kids, students, followed me everywhere. I don't think I'd ever want to be famous. There was just no privacy—it's the hardest thing to get used to. Plus, cultural mores are so different. I mean, there, the men wore a lungee, which is like a sarong, and the men squatted to urinate, they held hands, they picked flowers. I really thought this whole society is queer. That was my initial reaction, being a North American Yankee. I said, I can't take this.

But I didn't want . . . the other 12 [Peace Corps] people in Bangladesh were in villages all over the place. I said, I'm not going to be the first one to quit. That was the essential thing that kept me there for the first ninety days. I mean, I was so shook up the first day I was there that the shirt I wore—I don't know what kind of body odor I generated, but I never could get it out—I had to throw the shirt away. I was so traumatized. It was just so different.

When I went to the University of Chicago for training, I knew how to get my laundry cleaned. I knew how to get my next meal. I knew how to get home if I had to. When I was dropped off by the volunteer at my site in Bangladesh, it was sort of like, I don't know how to do anything really. I had training, and I knew it intellectually, but all of a sudden, there you are in a village, 12 thousand miles away from everything you knew as your home and your home culture—like I don't know how to take a bath. I don't know how or where to go to the bathroom. I don't know where to get food, how to feed myself. And then all these people—it was sort of like I was a movie star—all crowding around me. I couldn't even think. And, of course, they were just trying to be polite.

And then the whole idea of private property was entirely different there. It's much more communal. So when I'd go to settle in, for instance, all the students would come in and they'd be trying on my clothes and turning on my radio. When there'd be a break at lunch—we'd teach in the morning and then there'd be a long break until it would cool down and then we'd go back to class—and most people would take siestas. The students would come to my room. They'd be trying on my clothes and then walking out the door. At first I was really upset with it until I realized that's what everyone did. It wasn't that they were being impolite or that they were stealing. It's just that things are much more communal. They knew it was mine, but it would go off for three days with somebody else, and it would eventually come back. It was a whole different view of private property.

Joe, a Peace Corps volunteer in Southern India 1963-65, also remembers the lack of privacy:

When you went to sleep at night, your window would be filled with faces looking in, and when you woke up at first light in the morning it was still filled with faces looking in at you. There was no window shade. In the evening after supper, in our living room, if there were only eight or ten people, it meant there was some festival going on because there were so few people.

There is an Indian phrase, a very useful one—originally a religious phrase—"If you are simply in the presence of a great spirit, you gain merit." Good things happen to you just sitting quietly when somebody important is around.

Many of the villagers, particularly, they heard that there was this strange phenomenon—these Americans were living there—and they'd come and squat in the corner and sit there. You'd ask them, would you like some tea? Sometimes they'd say yes. We'd ask, is there anything we can do? They'd say no. The students would sit in chairs. The villagers weren't comfortable in chairs. They would sit on cushions on the floor. If you keep squatting all your life, it's very comfortable.

During this stage of the heroic journey—the departure stage—the process of detachment from the familiarity and comfort of home is deliberate and definite. Such a separation, as these recollections show, accelerates the young person's movement toward independence, both financial and emotional.

Encounter with the Guardian Spirit:
"Show me where to go, what to do"

Challenge: to be willing and open to learn
what is necessary for the challenge ahead,
to follow guidance.

None of us gets through life alone. The need for a guide is imperative, at certain times more so than at others. Points of transition in life make us vulnerable and in special need of someone or something to steer us on the right path. Traditional cultures built guidance into their rules, rituals, customs, and the "way things are always done." In addition, the elders were the bulwark in the passage ways of life. Furthermore, the young in many tribal cultures were encouraged to turn to their dreams and visions for inner guidance. Elders helped in their interpretation.

Mentoring is inherent to the elder's role in traditional cultures. In fact, the origin of the word "mentor" reveals some clues about its importance in adolescent development. The word goes back to the *Odyssey*.[3] As Odysseus is struggling to return home 10 years after the battle of Troy, his adolescent son Telemachus is struggling to enter adulthood. The goddess Athena, realizing that Telemachus must become a man if he is going to help his father on his return, appears to the young man in the guise of a family friend, Mentor. As Mentor, Athena—goddess of wisdom—will lead Telemachus through his heroic journey to adulthood. Note that feminine wisdom appears to the youth in the guise of a masculine figure—perhaps a warning that the journey depends on both feminine and masculine qualities.

In contrast, a culture like the United States where rugged individualism has been the leading value for two centuries, guidance is not so easy to come by. Except in tight-knit ethnic groups, rules, rituals, and customs do not carry the power in American culture that is evident in tribal cultures. Furthermore, in our culture the role of the elders is undefined and not understood. Everything in this culture tends to pull the young person's attention outward toward getting in touch with the latest music and pop culture, rather than inward toward getting in touch with inner resources. The question is, where is one to find guidance if it is no longer available in the traditional institutions: the church, the school, the community?

Former members of the youth corps give us some pointers in their memories of their own "guardianship" experiences in moving into their service experiences: that is, what moved them, what guided them in developing their inner resources, and who emerged as mentor figures for them.

Inner Guidance

Julie remembers a film that had a profound impact on her as a teenager and was to provide the momentum for her decision to join a service corps.

> At 15 I was awakened to possibilities in life. There was a TV movie on Jean Donovan who was one of the women who was murdered in El Salvador in 1980 or '81. There were four women murdered, three nuns and Jean Donovan. . . . I attended Catholic schools, and we were all aware of this horrific thing.
>
> I watched this movie and I was so struck because Donovan was portrayed as a very average girl. She had very basic average experiences. She had had dates and she had gone to college. She wasn't a saint. She wasn't someone who had just dropped out of the sky and was holy or anything. She was very normal. I related to her. I was very struck by her willingness to go away and do something and give of herself and just give up a lot of things she had had her whole life.
>
> I remember watching that movie and thinking, I want to do something like that. I may not be able to give my whole life. I don't know if I would want to be a martyr for anything, but I was really drawn to the idea that an average person can actually make a difference . . . or give something up. We don't have to live by the status quo that society says we have to have these things, that we have to get a good-paying job right out of college. It's much more important to be with other people, to serve, more than to wait to see what society is going to give us.

So Julie went to Alaska with the Jesuit Volunteer Corps.

Program Orientations

Julie describes her orientation:

> We had a week of JVC orientation in mid-August. All of
> the volunteers who would be in the Northwest section
> had an orientation at a camp right outside of Portland,
> Oregon. There were about 130 of us together with staff
> members.
>
> We had talks on the four criteria for JVC: simple life
> style, spirituality, community, and social justice. All
> during the week there was a variety of speakers. A
> Native American spoke about Native spirituality and
> culture. There were many jobs in the Northwest that
> were tailored to that population. People could learn
> about the populations they'd be working with. There
> were talks about alternative forms of spirituality: Yoga
> and meditation, for instance.
>
> We also dealt with living in community. Basically the
> JVC staff would say, "The most specific thing we can
> tell you is that community life is going to be the hardest
> thing you are going to have to endure." The most they
> could do was to give us suggestions.

Marjorie, who met her husband Steve when they
were both Peace Corps volunteers in Togo, West Africa,
during the mid '70s, remembers:

> They gave us enough [orientation] . . . but nothing could
> ever be enough . . . 'cause once you're out there on your
> own, that's when you learn the fastest. But I thought
> they did a good job. The orientation was in Togo, and
> that's important to do it in-country. We spent two and a
> half months—almost too long. You're not sworn in as a
> volunteer until the end of the orientation. There's plenty
> of time to say this is not for me, and the Peace Corps

sent you back with their blessing. They told us before
we ever left American soil that there is no way you can
know before you get there if this is going to work for
you or not.

Marjorie's and Steve's experiences in the early '70s
bore out the recommendation of Nate who underwent his
orientation in the early '60s at the University of Chicago
before he was sent to Bangladesh and then felt at a sudden
loss when he was in-country. Training on site was a
significant improvement in preparing the volunteers for the
reality of what they would face.

Emily remembers her orientation with the Lutheran
Volunteer Corps in Washington, D.C. [1991-92]:

During our orientation we were each given a dollar and
had to go find ourselves dinner. Some people just went
and bought a hot dog. I was in a group where we pooled
our money together and went to 7-Eleven and bought a
box of crackers and some cream cheese and Evian water;
so all of us had something to eat.

Some others went to Happy Hour and got something
like a Coke and the three appetizers that came with it.
And others got the 89 cent burger at McDonald's. Then
we came back together at the church and talked about it,
what we had done, and how it felt. I think someone even
gave their dollar away [thinking], "Tomorrow we're
going to have a nice breakfast. Tonight we're going
home to a nice bed."

Such experiences provide creative practice in
assessing available resources and making the best use of
them, something that young corps members will be
constantly challenged to do during their term of service.

An important aspect of the City Year orientation is the bonding process. Bill recalls their weekend together in western Massachusetts:

> It was at a retreat center on a lake in the mountains. . . It was nice . . . but intensive. You go in strangers, and you come out family. I think they were pretty effective in pulling that off. We did one afternoon of ropes course, a great way to break down a lot of inhibitions about meeting everyone. We did a service project as a whole group. It was something like trail clearing or trail building . . . definitely physical labor. A lot of time was spent talking about our families and our experiences and about what we wanted to get out of this. We did this in small groups, but the groups would switch around. We weren't assigned to our teams till the end.

The Partnership for Service-Learning, in addition to its week of orientation, adds a required academic component to the service experience—a course entitled Social Institutions. Don, who went to Ecuador, recalls why the course was so important for his own sense of well-being:

> Social Institutions helped me to see my work in a social context. Without that course I would have been overwhelmed with the amount of stimuli that you get on a daily basis. How do you reconcile this extreme poverty with your life in the United States and your upbringing? Some of my peers were working in orphanages and were seeing things they had never seen before, and it had high emotional impact.
>
> It's a dangerous thing to put idealistic students in a no-win situation. So if you don't address those issues, then it can be very destructive. The Social Institutions course helped us process all the experiences that we were

106

having by showing us the historical context, the economic system, the bigger picture of how Ecuador fits into the global picture. It gave us a formal time when we could discuss issues such as why things are the way they are and what is this process of an evolving society and what are some possible solutions. And I could go home—and the others could go home—feeling, okay, I can get up and go to work the next day knowing I'm not going to break down. I'm not going to be on stimulation-overload.

I have to give the directors a lot of credit. I mean, they could just throw you in somewhere and leave you to your own devices. It takes a lot of planning about which placements would be beneficial. It takes a lot of time to establish the community contacts. It's not an easy study-abroad program to implement.

For Don and his college peers the director of the service-learning program became a mentor during the time they were in Ecuador. This isn't always possible, however, where a program is large and time is brief.

Personal Mentors

Jim remembers who emerged as an important mentor for him in the CCC in the late 1930s:

The Forest Service at one point put me in charge of a big Schran compressor, with a bit grinder behind it, to drill holes in the highway. That was the Gunflint Trail. It had big boulders in it. We would dynamite them out and then level it out. That was my job.

There was a wonderful Army officer there. His name was Toomey. I asked him one day. I said, "What the heck is this gettin' me?" I don't know why I thought of that, an uneducated guy like I was.

And he says, "Jim, if nothing else, if you learn how to get along with your fellow man, whatever time you spent here will be worth it." He says, "You're maturing too."

True, I thought. I learned more about a lot of things in that time than I would ever learn in one year of college. I learned how to work with other people because, remember, on the farm you didn't do that. You worked pretty much alone. And I learned to be a leader, how to make tough decisions. I learned how to be a mechanic. I had to overhaul those trucks completely, keep them going, that sort of thing. 'Course I got to play baseball. After all this, it wasn't hard for me to go in the Navy during World War II. That was a breeze.

Marjorie also remembers, with great affection, her mentor in Togo when she was in the Peace Corps:

The director of the Peace Corps was a great father figure for me, very supportive of me and very supportive of my relationship with Steve. He and his wife watched us fall in love. That was very good for us to have them.

But, as helpful as most of the orientations were, there was a significant lack of strong personal mentors for the young corps members. A number of them said that those who should have been mentoring them—the staff members of the program—did not assume a very significant role. In many cases, sheer distance of the service site from the staff office prevented closer interaction. In some instances staff members were not adequately trained to mentor the volunteers; in other instances they lacked the people-skills. In several cases the young corps members found their mentor in-country in an older member of the indigenous community. Joe remembers his Peace Corps experience in southern India and who it was that stepped in to serve that role for him when he was working on his poultry project:

> The fellow who was the secretary of the poultry cooperative was actually a translations clerk in the government justice department. But he put most of his energy into this chicken business. He was very helpful. I would go over to his house. We'd have coffee together in the morning and talk.
>
> And then there was a young poultry development officer. I spent quite a bit of time at his house as well. You'd always get invited to people's houses. But I discovered, it's one thing to function in a business in a foreign language, quite another to be casual and intimate in another language. This made their patience and kindness all the more notable.

Nate remembers the point at which the headmaster of his school in Bangladesh made the transition from being his boss to becoming his friend and mentor:

> I had been there just about three months. We had a holiday. My headmaster invited me to come home with him to his village, which I thought was very nice. I went. During dinner there had been a hurricane. There was no electricity. We were just settling down after dinner when all of a sudden one of his little daughters comes over. She couldn't have been more than six-years-old. She comes over and starts rubbing my skin. He says, "Don't be surprised. She has never seen a white person before."

I think that invitation was a breakthrough because it cemented a relationship between the headmaster and me. He began to see me more as a friend, someone that at least he could confide in as opposed to someone that might be there to impose something on him. It was at that point that I began to feel that I might be able to make it.

Deliah, who spent two years with her husband Fred in the Jesuit International Volunteers in Belize, recalls with great affection:

We had the JIV grandmom, Miss Olive, who lived across the street from us. She's a Creole woman, about 85 now. If I had a bad day at school, I would just sit with her and talk about it. She was always a big help to me. She has been a kind of grandmother to the JIVs since the program first came there 10 years ago.

Ruth, the single mother who became a VISTA, recalls that her mentoring came not only from her work supervisor but also from the women who lived near her:

My housing complex—I hate to say project, because that's the negative stereotype—was small. It used to be military housing. We considered ourselves a neighborhood. Everybody knew everybody. We would check on each other. People knew that I was the woman that went to work every day at the soup kitchen.

When it came time for me to leave, they were so proud of me: "You finally got out of here." There was a sense of community there. Yet there was also at times a sense of isolation because some people felt that it was the only place they were going to be, and they just had to make the best of it. So you had the good and the bad.

The varied experiences indicate that the guardian spirit may be expressed in one or more of several ways: 1)as a spiritual awakening—perhaps a dream or strong intuition or even a film—which was the case with Julie who was deeply moved by the story of Jean Donovan; 2)as an orientation for a new phase of life, as was the case of Emily in the Lutheran Volunteer Corps, and Steve and Marjorie in the Peace Corps in Togo; 3)perhaps by an actual person—a mentor who develops a personal relationship and sense of responsibility toward the youth—as was the case of Joe and his colleagues in the poultry cooperative and of Nate with his headmaster in Bangladesh and of Deliah with Miss Olive in Belize; or yet a community of people, as was the case with Ruth.

Ideally, all three expressions of guardianship will be present in the lives of our young people: the spiritual awakening, an effective orientation for the new stage of life, and caring mentors. But the reality is that many of us can and do make the passage with only one or, at most, two of such forms of guardianship. All the more reason for a variety of possibilities to be strengthened by the community at large so that all young people will have access to at least some form of guardianship.

Loretta, who went with the American Friends Service to post-W.W.II Germany, discovered how devastating it can be when walking into a shocking situation, such as the war destruction presented to her in 1947, and finding absolutely no adult guidance. She recalls:

> We arrived in London and went to a Friends' Center
> where we had to wait before we could go over to
> Germany. It was all very exciting. But when we landed
> in Hanover, I saw a world that was razed to the ground.
> It was much worse than I had ever anticipated. I was so

horrified, I had to go to bed. All I could do was weep the first three days. There was no one I could turn to.

The gulf between young people and older adults is especially bleak during times of trauma, but research tells us how little personal contact there is between adolescents and adults in the most ordinary of times.[4] Age segregation is as serious, if more subtle, a problem as racial segregation. Yet, until we recognize that we—young and old—need each other, this kind of segregation will continue.

Nevertheless, there is an encouraging sign: Mentoring (or mentorship) is becoming the catchword of the decade. More than simple good-will is needed, however, for such a complex and important relationship.[5] After all, it is the guardian spirit—whatever form it takes—that will beckon the young people from their old lives into the place of their initiation. Still, as anxious as the young are to move into this new stage, they may soon wonder, "What did I get myself into?"

* * *

Chapter Five

Initiation:
"This wasn't what I bargained for."

The youth has heard and responded to the call, made the decision to depart from home and all that was familiar, found some sort of guidance on the path, and has now entered a "betwixt and between" period of life. This is where extraordinary things can happen, where he will be called on to do tasks he never thought were possible, where she will be stretched to the limit, where they both will achieve victory if they endure the challenge. But it can be a tough time, usually not what they bargained for.

The tribal youngster quickly becomes aware that he or she is not in this thing (i.e., the rite of passage) alone. Not only is the whole community involved—mother, father, siblings, extended family, neighbors and friends—but one's ancestors. The whole cosmic force comes face-to-face with the young initiate and validates his or her existence. In view of such evidence, a youngster cannot deny her own value, nor can he turn his back on the task or ordeal ahead, which may include fasting, circumcision, scarring of the face or body, knocking out or filing certain teeth, or tattooing. In addition to proving personal courage and strength in the face of such an ordeal, he must uphold the reputation of his whole family by acting with dignity and pride.

The contemporary youngster, in contrast, often feels alone and isolated in his and her risky adventure unless aided and abetted by peers who are likely feeling just as alienated. They may be saying to themselves, "This isn't what I bargained for!"

Taking on the Task:

"What did I get myself into?"

Challenge: to make a commitment to a task
that transcends personal boundaries
and to persevere in it.

F or both the young man and the young woman in tribal
culture, the task, the ordeal, and the victory are
clearly defined within the context of their community
ritual. For the young man and woman in contemporary
American society, this initiation process is not so evident.

Defining the Task

Using contemporary youth service as an example of the
journey, we find the vital task phase sometimes too loosely
outlined. Early Peace Corps members and Volunteers in
Service to America (VISTA) frequently would arrive at
their assigned sites only to discover that there was no job
description. They were left to create their own.[1]

Joe, a Peace Corps volunteer in 1963, remembers:

I was sent to southern India. It was fairly early in the
Peace Corps and tasks were somewhat vaguely defined.
I was sent there to be a youth worker, whatever that was.
Supposedly somebody had talked to somebody about
organizing youth clubs in villages. Culturally the
Indians aren't into youth clubs. Several decades later I

would still fit their definition of youth. A youth is someone in an Indian village who doesn't have control over the land yet. Men retain control over the land as long as they're alive. There are plenty of 55-year-old "youth" because their father was still alive and very much hanging onto control. So they were treated as youth.

I discovered there was a small government subsidy for youth clubs in villages. Youth clubs had a tendency to form long enough to collect this subsidy and then disappear. It didn't amount to much. It was around $15.

Like many of us in those days, we began to figure out what was there to do that would make sense. I spent some time working with the agricultural extension program there and then got involved particularly with chickens. From a Peace Corps member's perspective, poultry is a very attractive thing. Chickens grow up and mature and produce a "crop" within a two-year period. In fact, less than that. You can get a "crop" of broilers in about nine weeks. You get chickens laying eggs in a year. So we founded a poultry cooperative society in the area.

Like many other early Peace Corps volunteers, Joe designed his own task to fit the specific needs of the area. Married couples, however, had their own special challenges. If only one spouse in the couple found a good fit of skills to task, that often meant the other spouse would be mismatched. Dave and Libby's experience is an example. They married while undergrad students and went into the Peace Corps right after graduation in 1967. Dave, who majored in architecture, insisted that his work assignment be in his field. It was. He designed buildings in Tunis.

Libby, who had majored in geology and had experience working in the soil lab while a student, hoped to make use of her training. Unfortunately, she inherited a job that had been created by young women who had preceded her to Tunisia. As Libby describes it,

> A bunch of kindergarten teachers had been sent over to teach kindergarten to the peasants' four- and five-year-olds, which would prepare them to . . . what? There wasn't any school to go to. So these women turned their project into a birth control program so they could stay there.

> I followed them up in the birth control program. It was horrendously boring. I had no one to talk to and no friends. I would give a little garbled speech in Arabic to a bunch of ladies. They were always the same. They would come back every week. There aren't that many people in Tunisia. Their story is, "I'm 16 years old. I have so many children." It wasn't a very happy situation. Muslim culture believes in early marriages.

> It was unfortunate the way the program was set up. Here I am, this western woman who is considered a harlot in the first place, with her outrageous mode of clothes and her funny accent and weird behavior. And I am supposed to tell these ladies how to implement birth control, which is something they don't want to hear about because it's antithetical to their whole culture.

> A year after we left, the program was discontinued. But, reflecting back, I think that the family planning program did have some effect. In fact, some of the women with 10 or 12 children did elect to have the [sterilization] operation, which was one of the options.

However the task is defined—by the corps, by a work supervisor, or by the young person herself—what is essential is purpose: that what she is doing makes sense, that it not be mere busy-work. Nothing turns young people into cynics faster than entrapment in make-work. On the other hand, nothing evokes heroic qualities more effectively than engagement in necessary work.

Dave adds:

> I was lucky enough to insist on and land a location
> where buildings were being designed and built, so I did
> practice architecture. I went to a place that was the local
> office of the Division of Subdivisions and Roads and
> Buildings and Bridges. It was a tongue-twisting title in
> Arabic. There were five or six draftsmen. There were
> two engineers and one architect from Bulgaria, with
> whom Tunisia traded. A French-trained Tunisian headed
> the office. We did a lot of buildings. The Bulgarians
> pretty much had their own projects, but I used the
> Bulgarian structural engineer for my projects.

Libby perceived little purpose in her work, Dave a great deal in his. Libby, however, would be the first to admit that the rewards of the experience went far beyond the task.

Dealing with the Difficult

Often the difficulty of the task ahead becomes apparent fairly quickly. Jim remembers his task with the CCC in the late '30s, which involved leading a team of rough eastern European immigrants from upper Minnesota:

> I was planting trees. Most of the guys were from the
> Iron Range where they mine the iron up in northern
> Minnesota: Yugoslavs, Croatians, Finlanders, they were

118

supposed to be awful tough. You worked in a line, and the best worker worked in front. He worked first; [dropping his voice] that was me. No one could outwork me [laughing]; it was competitive.

Well, I did that for about a month. Then they realized that I might be a little brighter than some of the others, so they put me to surveying with a forester, going from section to section, marking what kind of trees were in it. Balsam and birch over pine trees, for instance. If that was the case, they were going to get rid of the balsam and birch 'cause that was a junk tree up there. They wanted evergreens, spruce, white pine, so on. So you made a map of all this. That was really great 'cause you were working with a compass, a rod, and a chain.

Doris too (the Red Cross nurse) discovered all too soon how difficult her task would be, situated as she was, near the front lines of World War II:

Since we were very close to the front, we would move about every week or every five days as the battle lines moved. If there was a building standing we would be assigned there to create our hospital. Usually these buildings were filthy dirty so we had to clean them up before we could start taking care of patients. Otherwise we would have to pitch tents. During the winter it was bitter cold. [She shivers at the memory.]

When Nate went to Bangladesh in the 1960s, he realized that teaching biology was one thing but teaching biology in Bengali quite another. He remembers his first five minutes in the classroom thinking he was in no way prepared to handle this task:

The headmaster said to me, "I want you to go into this classroom." The headmaster spoke English, although when I got in the classroom, of course, it was all in Bengali. I had learned Bengali during my orientation, or so I had thought. And I was teaching students, some of whom were learning English as part of their curriculum, but they couldn't speak English well at that point. And all the teachers taught in Bengali.

So, here I go into a science class, it was a biology class. They gave me a textbook. It was in Bengali. Well, I wasn't in there more than five minutes, and it was obvious that I was in no way ready to take over a class. So the headmaster pulled me back out. It kind of shook me up. I thought, Gosh, if I'm going to have to start teaching like this tomorrow I'm not fit to do this job.

But this is what happened. That first year I worked with teachers, helping them with equipment and doing the demonstration. They did the teaching. I assisted in the labs. Then my second year there I actually started teaching classes on my own. It was still difficult. It took a lot of preparation. Students could still throw questions at me, and I would have to do research in Bengali before I could answer them.

Marjorie and Steve, who met as Peace Corps Volunteers in Togo, West Africa in the mid-'70s, both taught English in their respective villages. A typical class was 60 students. When Marjorie ended up one term with a class of only 40, she thought she was in heaven.

Steve, whose students ranged from 12 to 19 years old, remembers:

There was electricity in the main building of the school but none in the classrooms. So whatever light you got came in through the squares in the cinder blocks. Usually it was so sunny, you got enough light, but if it was a rainy day, you couldn't see the blackboard. You couldn't see anything. So you'd do dictates. You'd do oral reports. If it rained too hard, it was impossible to teach because you couldn't hear a thing.

Marjorie recalls:

There were no textbooks. You'd put everything on the board. The students had little bitty notebooks to write in and had to put everything into the notebooks. Togo has since moved away from Americans teaching Togolese students toward teaching Togolese teachers, which seems to make more sense.

For Ben, it was grossly inappropriate textbooks rather than a lack of textbooks which he faced when he went to northern Iran with the Peace Corps. His task in 1962 was to teach English at an agricultural training center. In dealing with that situation, he came to realize that challenges were opportunities:

Another Peace Corps volunteer and I were assigned together to this school. Our students were 16 to 25-year-old village youth, who were going through 9th, 10th, and 11th grades. A small group of them would actually go on and finish 12th grade. The rest would return to their village and become teachers in elementary schools. So there were a lot of different things in the curriculum. I taught English and my Peace Corps buddy taught P.E.

But it wasn't that simple. I didn't understand Islam. I didn't understand any of the politics that were going on in the country. I understood that I was supposed to be an English teacher, but I wasn't trained as a teacher. I had studied American poetry, and it's one thing to write a paper on Hart Crane and quite another to teach a class of sixty 16 to 25-year-olds who can barely read and write Persian, let alone speak English.

My initial text, provided by the government, was
Gulliver's Travels. So here I am, trying to teach
Gulliver's Travels in Persian and thinking, This isn't
working very well. So I just threw all that stuff away
and began designing my own materials because I didn't
know what else to do.

My buddy became frustrated and asked to be reassigned
to another part of the country. My approach, on the other
hand, has always been, if things went wrong, well,
things went wrong. I tried not to be frustrated by events,
because people had said, "Look, you're going into an old
culture, it's been around a long time. Don't expect to
conquer the world overnight."

Seizing Opportunities. The Peace Corps gave each of
us a footlocker of books. I was going to read as much as
I possibly could. I was going to learn the language well,
and I was going to try to be as useful as I could to the
principal of our school who was willing to have a couple
of Americans working there.

This principal also set me up with two high schools in
town: a boys' high school and a girls' high school, which
was great for me. I'd ride my bicycle 10 miles into town
and teach in these schools a couple of times a week. He
also set me up as the tutor to the son of the governor.
The governor and his wife had been educated in
America. Their son spoke a little English, but they
wanted him to continue practicing. So one hour a week I
did that.

I also took advantage of situations. I had swum
competitively in high school and college. The
opportunity opened up in Iran to teach swimming at a
Boy Scout camp the following summer after the school
year. I also helped train the national Olympic team. You
hear about things and you think, Can I help?

In my second year some Presbyterian missionaries established a foundation to train Armenian and Assyrian girls who were a minority in Iran. These girls were very bright and knew that if they could get English they could get a job, and they could move on up in society. So I helped set up the school. Some people in Tehran were developing a first-rate English text, and we were the first people to experiment with it. It was great. You know, you take advantage of situations to the extent that you can.

Ben not only kept his eyes open for opportunities, but he made use of his own resources to help in whatever ways he could.

Using the Resources

A critical part of the task of all of the young corps members is learning how to find, to assess, and to make effective use of available resources. Emily, with the Lutheran Volunteer Corps, remembers this as her greatest challenge in working with the homeless in Washington, D.C. in 1991:

I was an outreach worker with the homeless. I helped them move on to a better life by connecting them with appropriate services. The most challenging part of my job for the first six months was figuring out all the services: what were government services, what were private services, what services were there under all these acronyms, who was who in the government and in the service-provider community—all very confusing in the beginning.

Carol, who joined VISTA in 1970, had to create her own task because her supervisor had no idea what she was supposed to do when she arrived in Montana. She also had to train herself to identify and access resources:

> I was actually assigned to the governor's office in Helena, Montana. I was an ombudsman for the Native American population at the state Department of Indian Affairs. There were seven large Indian reservations and several urban Indian communities in the state. It was one of those indefinite assignments. After a few weeks with no direction from the supervisor, I decided the best thing I could do was figure out how to bring money into the state for the Native American population.
>
> So I got out the catalog on domestic assistance and worked my way diligently through all the organizations that offered funding. After that, I kind of did a circuit riding thing and created a network of VISTAs on the other reservations. Then I figured out how to do one application. My goal was to have all seven reservations apply for everything that was available. There were like 328 potential funding sources. I think I worked my way through six in a year's period.
>
> Except for being able to think and write, there was nothing in my college background to help me in this. My major was political science, which was very theoretical. It gave me no insights into political structures in the real world.

For Ed in Nigeria during the 1950s, his background in mathematics provided the skills to evaluate the sources of water. He recalls:

> On arrival, about 15 of the students were in the hospital with bilharzia, a snail-borne disease that gets to your

intestines. It comes from drinking water from a polluted stream where the snails live. I saw a little trickle of water coming out of the ground of a hillside on the campus. The principal didn't think there was enough there to be useful. I got a stopwatch from the lab and a bucket and calculated how much there would be and found out there was over 600 gallons a day, plenty for 300 boys and staff members. So he said, "Okay, we'll try it out." We went up to Ibadan [university] to get it tested.

The challenge sometimes went beyond identifying and accessing resources to that of multiplying the resources. Joe describes what inspired him in India in the '60s:

Those early weeks were difficult. I can remember feeling very down. And then the first time that the Peace Corps director came to visit my area, he invited me to go around the state with him. When we got to a little town up in the northern part of the state, there was another volunteer whom I'd known very well in training. We spent two days there.

This volunteer had gotten into a poultry thing similar to my situation. He was granted some leave and went up to visit some volunteers in northern India who were also doing this and brought back a lot of their manuals and stuff and was in the process of getting them translated. I remember thinking, We could do that.

When I came back from that experience, I built this chicken house and bought these chickens. That's when I realized that the available chicken feed was killing the chickens, and we had to find a way to get decent chicken feed.

In fact, I made it up in my own back room first to see if it would work. I would make it in thousand-pound batches. It involved some time up at the university figuring out what chicken feed is made of, then finding out where you can buy the stuff. Then you were always adjusting it because sometimes you couldn't get this thing and sometimes that. We had to find sources of things, which was pretty tricky because there was a lot of food shortage at that time.

Crucial to the project was finding a mill where they brought in U.S. AID [Agency for International Development] wheat to be ground. They ran it through a sieve before they got it there. The ships they brought it over in had corn in them before, so there was a fair amount of corn they sieved out of the wheat, and they sold that real cheap. The reason you could get it cheap was that it was about three-quarters corn, about 20% stones and sticks and about 5% nails. So you had to go over it kernel by kernel. I hired two women, paid them a rupee a day, plus the nails (15 cents a day, plus they could take home the nails). They were so happy because they were getting a couple of rupees worth of nails a day. The standard wage for women was a rupee a day; for men it was a rupee and a quarter.

I bought another batch of chickens, and they did fine on this feed. In addition to the feed, though, you had to go out and find out where they sold the right kind of vitamins and figure out how you could get the right mix and not get vitamins that were light-sensitive. But there were people around who knew all of that.

Steve, during the '70s, brought some resources from home to his Peace Corps site in Togo:

I took a "ton" of Frisbees with me, and everywhere I went I showed them how to play. It was just a little Frisbee diplomacy. The kids loved it. The terrain is real barren there . . . great for Frisbee!

126

Deliah brought the series of *The Little House on the Prairie* books with her when she went to Belize in the late '80s as a Jesuit Volunteer to teach in a school for disadvantaged girls:

> A lot of the girls had learning disabilities or behavioral problems. So it was kind of the last chance high school for the young women of Belize. My assignment was teaching what they call first form. It's the British system. It was comparable to our freshman year of high school.

> You will see why *Little House on the Prairie* was important in a moment. My first year I had a class of 30. My second year I was given the remedial class. I always called them the remedials of the remedials because all of the girls were catching up for what they missed in primary school.

> There was no syllabus. The students had no books. It was a self-contained classroom. I taught all the subjects: reading, spelling, math, history, science, health, religion, everything. I didn't have much staff support from the faculty. I didn't have anybody offering me critiques. I kind of just had to go on my instinct.

> Having been in school most of my life, I had some models of teaching in my mind. The teacher-training during orientation also helped. It doesn't seem like much, but it was more than I had before. That gave me a structure to use. I learned some discipline techniques, some planning . . . so that was helpful.

> But I always felt that my biggest task in working at that school was to give the young women some sense of self-esteem. They had never heard that they had done

anything well. I would pick the littlest thing out and try to make a big deal of it.

Anyway, *Little House on the Prairie* was important to me as I was growing up. I guess it was that Midwestern pioneering spirit. (I'm from Nebraska, and as far as my group of friends and my family, I was kind of a pioneer.) I got several sets of those books and brought them down to Belize with me and read them with the students. My second Christmas I got enough books to give them each a copy and told them to share them. These books helped me make a connection with the girls.

Connecting with the Community

In the process of transcending personal boundaries in confronting the task, the young person becomes aware of the necessity of interdependence[2] with a community in order to accomplish the task. Joe depended on the animal husbandry and poultry development officers for his region in India to help him develop the poultry cooperative, as well as on the agricultural college where he could take his questions about poultry pathology. It would have been impossible for him to accomplish what he did without this kind of assistance.

Carol discovered in 1970 that building her network of Native American friends and VISTA peers on the Montana reservations helped her work more effectively in the capital. Because she was a couple of years older than many of her peers, she created another "task" for herself, that of counselor and "den mother" in charge of maintaining morale. Younger VISTAs would come to spend a few days with her in her city apartment for a little R&R when they needed it. They helped her; she was a support for them.

Nate could not have survived his first year in Bangladesh in the 1960s without the guidance of his fellow Bengali teachers. As a teaching and lab assistant, he followed their lead and learned from them enough to step into his full task as a classroom teacher by his second year.

Emily learned in the early '90s that there is a supportive network "out there" for the homeless in Washington, D.C., but she had to develop the knowledge and skills to access it. It became evident to her that she was not in this work alone, that she was but a small part of an enormous whole, working together to solve, or at least to alleviate, some of the most difficult urban problems.

Next to acknowledging the importance of working with—and ultimately depending on—fellow human beings, is recognizing the importance of resources: what they are, where to find—or how to create—them, how to use them wisely, and how to conserve them. When you get right down to it, these are the most notable characteristics of maturity: the recognition of the interdependence of all life, and the wise use of resources.[3]

A paradox is at work here. At the same time the young person is becoming independent, she is also coming to realize she is profoundly interdependent. But what is significant is that he has moved from an unconscious and assumed dependence on his parents and immediate family to a conscious and appreciative interdependence with the wider community.

In the City Year experience, this process takes the form of team-building, an essential part of taking on the task.[4] Bill, who was with City Year in '90-91, remembers:

> There were 11 of us: two black guys, three black girls,
> an Hispanic girl, two white girls, two white guys,
> something like that. A pretty good mix. At the time,
> City Year was pretty specifically for Boston area people,

but in our group I was from D.C. Another girl was from
Arizona, one from New York. So there was a
geographic mix.

But there was another kind of mix as well. You have
kids coming out of Exeter and Andover—they've lived
the prep school existence all their lives. And then you
have kids put there by the courts. I mean, that's an
interesting combination. It's very good in some
respects; but in terms of functionality, it's a real
challenge.

Members of the religion-based corps—such as the
Brethren, Jesuit, Lutheran, and Mennonite—had their
challenges too. They faced another "task," in addition to
their assigned job: the challenge of living with a community
of people.

Emily recalls the significance of her community-
living experience with three other women in the Lutheran
Volunteer Corps:

Each house or community was supposed to form a
covenant incorporating their ideas into a kind of mission
statement—how they intended to live in their
community. For instance, how much time they would
share together; whether or not they would be
accountable to each other by being there for each other
and sharing.

It was a difficult thing for me because although
community seemed really great—"oh, this is so much
fun sort of thing"—actually it's also a challenge. I'm
someone who doesn't easily talk about my feelings, and
a lot of sharing was expected. At first, I was the really
quiet one and so I felt kind of selfish. Inside I felt really
challenged at our house meetings when they were just

sharing times. I was really challenged to be tolerant and patient, to share a part of myself with others.

So, along with the task, comes the opportunity to transcend personal boundaries. This may be the first time the young American takes on a project for a purpose other than getting a grade or earning a paycheck. The discovery of other rewards for a job well done gives hints that life may be something more than commercial exchange.

The Battle with the Beast:
"I can't handle it . . . help!

Challenge: to develop the courage to deal
with environmental dangers
but ultimately to face the dangers
of one's own perceived limitations
and to break through them.

Having undertaken the challenge and become engaged in the task, the young person comes face-to-face with the ordeal—the physical and emotional dangers—and ultimately comes to recognize his or her own perceived limitations or peer-imposed limitations. Often there is a feeling of being overwhelmed, of being stretched to the limit, of being caught in an impossible situation. Yet it usually is only at the moment when the youth is stretched to the limit that a breakthrough can be made.

Environmental Challenges

The new environment often holds sights, sounds, and dangers for the young corps member that can be frightening and physically draining. Jim remembers the "beast" in his CCC experience:

> The big fires came. The last big fire in this part of the country was in 1936. A huge wall of fire came down from Canada—late July and all of August and part of September. Then it rained. Our job was to stop the fire right on the U.S. border. There's a chain of lakes there with a stream between them, so what we would do is try to stop it at the lake. A fire was considered harmful in those days so you stopped it. They made me a leader in fighting fire. The Forest Service went out and recruited men from off the streets in Superior, Wis. and Duluth, Minn. and brought them up there and forced them to fight fire. That was not unusual.
>
> Here I am now, 18 years of age, and I was made the boss of about 30 of these guys. And they didn't want to work. And, of course, I was really a tough guy at that time; [laugh; then, more seriously] I was a tough kid. And I would make fools out of them, really, by just showing them how much work could be done with a mattock. I got 'em to work, so I was now made a leader. When we finished with the fires, I came back, and the Forest Service now expected to make me a leader in their woods.

It's probably a toss-up which was the worst danger, the fire or the work crew that Jim had to lead. Either way, the experience demanded every ounce of courage and acting ability to put on the brave, tough front day after day in order to accomplish the job.

For Doris, nursing as she was at the front in World War II, her first experience of the shelling was terrifying:

> I remember it was in France where we joined the battle lines. Shelling was going on all around us. Having come from South Dakota where we had a lot of thunder storms, I thought, Gee, if I just think that we're having a thunder storm like back home, it won't be so bad. . . . I soon discovered that didn't help. We all ended up in a basement of a nearby building [for protection]. That was my initiation, my first encounter with real war.
>
> We were very young. It was hard to see the wounded soldiers day in and day out. There was no respite. We saw them dying all the time for months on end. There were only five nurses to each unit. We were working 12 hours on and 12 hours off. Frequently we moved at night. So you might be up for 24 hours. Thank God, there would be lapses in the battle when we could catch our breath.

Those scenes from 50 years ago are never far from the surface of Doris's memory.

For Julie, in the Jesuit Volunteer Corps, coming as she did from the U. S. South, the Alaskan winter was her "beast":

> The climate [in Alaska] was an enormous challenge. Coming from Tennessee and going to college in New Orleans, I had never been around so much snow before. Tremendous amounts of snow covered the ground from mid-October till the end of March. Everything is white. It was about mid-March when I was waiting for the bus to go home. I saw snowflakes in the air and thought, Oh no, if it snows one more time, I'll get the next plane back to Tennessee. I had just about reached the breaking point.

Another challenge was the mosquitoes. They were lethal—big and pervasive. But I must admit they were not as bad in the city as in the rural areas, thank goodness! But when I look back now I realize the incredible natural beauty more than made up for the rough stuff like snow and mosquitoes. The mountains—stunning! And the moose—huge! Because my winter there had the heaviest snow in years, the moose were wandering into the cities looking for food. What an experience to look out your window and see this gigantic animal strolling across your front yard.

Bill faced a different kind of challenge in Boston with City Year:

> Every time it rained we had to go to the Charlestown projects and clean elderly people's apartments. So if it was raining when you woke up in the morning, you knew where you were going.

> I remember this one rainy day two girls on my team had to go into the apartment of an elderly woman. This lady had thrown all of her dirty laundry for months into the bathtub and then proceeded to go to the bathroom on it. So not only are there roaches . . . and . . . I mean . . . they had to clean the bathroom . . . Then to do the laundry, they had to haul it down the street to the Laundromat. So we were dealing with some tough, tough living conditions in some of these apartments.

> So anyway, a couple weeks later it rains and down we go to the projects again. I was team leader assistant that week. I had to give out note cards with the cleaning assignments to my team members. Each card had the person's name, the address, and what we should expect. I got this one card. It was, like, "Roy something-or-other." I forget the last name. "Extremely dangerous.

Please wear gloves." I tried to give the card away to somebody else on my team. They wouldn't take it. They were, like, "You take it." So I say, "All right."

So I'm going into this apartment with an "extremely dangerous" warning. I don't know what to expect. I walk in there, imagining the worst. The place is spotless. I'm, like, "Roy, what do you want me to do?" He says, "Nothing." There's nothing to do. I sit down. He makes me breakfast. After that, anytime I went to the projects, I'd just go visit Roy. He'd tell me World War II stories. I don't know where that warning came from. I went in there thinking the worst, and it turned out to be great.

Both Bill and the girls on his team learned to garner their courage to face some pretty difficult conditions. In this case, however, Bill discovered his expectation was far worse than the reality. He also recognized that cleaning up a mess wasn't the only need of the elderly in the projects. A friend who will just listen counts too.

Perceived Limitations

Carol, who served her VISTA term in Montana in the early '70s, describes what for her was the beast:

I hated being poor. Never having any options. Having to think very, very, carefully before going to a movie, before buying anything—ANYTHING—be it food or whatever. That was probably my biggest learning experience, learning to live on our meager stipend. You were expected to live on the stipend that was provided so you would understand what it was like to live as a low-income person. That was the expectation of VISTA.

One of the young married couples—their parents did fly them home at Christmas. The rest of us did not go anywhere that year. I certainly did not. It was the first Christmas that I ever didn't. You couldn't live on the stipend and buy airline tickets at the same time. That was the idea: you were going to live on a poverty wage. For the VISTAs who were living in a closer knit community than mine, I think that was real important. Of course, most of them lived in some kind of housing provided by the project. We in the city did not have that benefit. Obviously the governor's office did not have any subsidized housing.

One of the values that VISTA hoped to transmit was that being poor sucks! It's very hard to live that way. It's grinding. It's demeaning. It's narrowing. You have no options. You only have enough resources to attend to the very basic things in life. Fortunately, I came into that year with adequate clothing. I certainly did not buy any during the course of that year. I couldn't have. But that was only one year of my life. For people in poverty, it's every year of their lives. My god, it's stultifying. How did they ever carve out that little bit of extra to get a pair of boots? And I can assure you that in Montana a pair of boots are important things.

I knew at the end of that long Montana winter my boots were dying and that if I were truly poor and knew that I were going to be poor for the next year and the next year and the next year, I would have been frantic. But I knew that wasn't the case. And I knew that I could leave and that my life would change. And that lesson has served me well whenever there are policy arguments about increasing benefits at the federal level or the state level. I am always painfully aware of how little value money really has.

For Erika, the meager stipend did not compare with the concern for personal safety. She remembers dealing with her parents' fears—and her own—about her life in Washington, D.C. with the Mennonite Volunteer Corps. This was a far different world than her farm life back home in Iowa:

> At first I think it was very difficult for my parents to see me here in Washington, D.C., in such a big city where people are . . . you know, all the violence and crime. When they came out to visit me once—actually it was the very first time when they left me off here my very first year, and it was up in Columbia Heights—they were leaving very early in the morning . . . it was like four in the morning. There was a cop out front that had somebody held up, you know, their hands were up and they were frisking them—right out the front door. Of course, I didn't see them then. And my parents called me later and said, "Erika, we're not so sure about this."

> I don't blame them. It was really frightening. If I were to say something to try to ease their mind, it would be to ease mine too, 'cause I was really scared. You kind of downplay it and say, "I try and be as cautious as I can be." But since then I haven't always told them everything I see and everything I do because . . . you just don't.

In a sense, Erika had been prepared for her challenging times in D.C. by her earlier experience with a college service program. As a senior, Erika spent a semester in Costa Rica, and came to terms with another of her "beasts":

> I was really insecure about the language in Costa Rica. That was a big thing. And I was constantly getting on myself and saying, "Oh yeah, you can't do this . . . you

can't speak," and feeling really bad about it. But I guess I was down there long enough that in order to survive I just had to do it [to speak the language]. My crisis point came in the refugee camp where I worked. There was a variety of reasons why it was really difficult. For one thing, I was this "rich, white Gringa" from the States and I had nice—they weren't nice clothes—but to them everything I wore or did was nice—and it made me feel very self-conscious. And I would walk into the camp and they would yell "Gringa, Gringa!"

The woman I worked with, she was Costa Rican, and all the refugees were Nicaraguan. She was very condescending to them and, I thought, really rude. I was just really struggling, trying to understand her and how she was treating them and not judge her because I was really angry with her and how she was treating everyone. I thought, well, maybe I don't understand culturally, maybe I shouldn't make these kinds of judgments.

I remember being angry with her and one day just crying for a variety of reasons 'cause she was treating me in the same way: like "You stupid person. You don't know Spanish well enough to be working here . . . do this . . . do that." And she'd call me "negra," which is "black." It's a very condescending thing to call someone. It made me very angry. It was not an easy time.

A lot of people [peers from college]—this was their first time out of country. The language was hard. It's exhausting to be in a place where you can't speak. I remember going to bed at 8 o'clock every night because my head is so full, I can't handle it. This is what a friend wrote in her journal, "I'm really tired. I miss home." And her advisor's comment was, "Grow up!" The fact is, she was trying to. We all were. This is the point of having students go down there. We were all trying to grow. That should have been acknowledged.

The Beasts Can Teach

What becomes evident is that site supervisors require training to work more effectively with their youthful volunteers. They can be powerful mentors and models, or they can demoralize their young assistants with sarcasm and disparaging remarks.

Erika's experience shows how an effective "guardian spirit" could have supported her and her peers. No program is immune to throw-away remarks by thoughtless adults that have a devastating effect on young people. But this was only one experience. Two people, an American advisor and an in-country supervisor, are not meant to be read universally. What it does indicate, however, is that every program needs constant vigilance and thorough training for its staff members.

Yet young people are resilient. They can learn, even from negative experiences, if other positive factors are in place. In the very best program there will be circumstances and people that are not ideal. It's best to be up-front about that from the beginning with the corps members and to find ways to inoculate them during the orientation to the less-than-ideal situations they may well encounter. Erika's own experience, in turn, has made her especially sensitive to the needs of the women in the urban shelter where she is now employed.

Steve and Marjorie, who met in the Peace Corps and later married, found a variety of hurdles in Togo as volunteers in the mid-'70s. But language wasn't one of them, even though Togo is a French-speaking nation. They both spoke French, each having spent time in France studying the language. They also took on the challenge of learning the local languages although they didn't have to. So the language, for them, was not a major problem. Other things, however, were.

Steve remembers his frustration with the "backwardness" of the people:

> On the weekends I would get on the motorcycle and go out to visit the villages of my students. They did all their agriculture by hand, just like they did a thousand years ago. Usually one kid would be picked to go to school because he had the desire or he was real smart. The rest of them had to stay on the farm.

> The living conditions seemed to be the same [as a thousand years ago] too. Everything was made out of sun dried mud. There was a well right next to them. So they worked really intensely for six months to plant and harvest, and then six months off. The families always lived together, so the grandmothers and grandfathers and parents and babies were all in the same compound. Everything went down to the lake to be laundered.

Marjorie had other concerns:

> What I never got used to was living in a country where I had to depend on drugs for my health . . . that I had to take anti-malaria pills . . . that I had to wash my vegetables in a chemical if I was going to eat them raw . . . that I had to boil and filter my water . . . this really weighed on me the whole time I was there. I wanted to get back to a country where I could drink water straight from the tap, or I could pick a peach and eat it and not have to worry about parasites and malaria all the time.

> My father's a doctor and was real concerned for my health. But I remember my parents saying, "Whatever

you want to do, that's fine with us." I thought that once they came to visit me, they would worry less, 'cause I knew they were concerned about me. On the contrary, after they visited me, they worried much more. They weren't worried about me in my ability to make good decisions—I remember my mother saying, "You seem to be in good control of your life."—but they were real worried for my health after they saw the country. It was much worse than they had imagined. By that time, I had grown so used to it, I wasn't able to see it through their eyes. When they were visiting me I didn't know how shocked they were. I only learned a few years ago how shocked they were.

The volunteers in Togo were given the use of motorcycles for daily transportation. Marjorie remembers her experience with her bike on her first day of living alone:

> I got off my motorcycle on the wrong side and got burned on the muffler . . . a big wound on the side of my leg. I was living alone so I had to take care of that all by myself. But I got one of the African women to help me with an aloe plant.

> Then later my place was robbed when I was out of town. I subsequently found out it was my landlord's son. I remember that revelation and how furious I was. What was happening to this wonderful image I had of Peace Corps life? Bad things were happening and I had to deal with it alone.

But Marjorie was yet to face the most difficult time of her life. She and Steve had met and fallen in love by this time. Their respective terms in Togo were coming to an end. Marjorie was at the Peace Corps office in the capital, looking forward to Steve meeting her there. He was on his way from his up-country site. Marjorie recalls what happened:

A telegram came into the office that read PEACE
CORPS VOLUNTEER ACCIDENT. CRANIAL
DAMAGE. SEND EMERGENCY MEDICAL CARE
IMMEDIATELY. Steve's taxi was in an accident and
overturned. It all took so long . . . watching them load
up blood plasma in the Land Rover . . . driving through
the mountains, over those rutted dirt roads. It seemed to
take forever . . . a good six or eight hours before we got
to him. And during that time I thought he was going to
die. And I envisioned flying back to the U.S. to meet his
mother for the first time with his coffin. We finally got
to the only hospital up-country. He had already been
operated on. And, yes, he survived.

For the first time in my life I realized that I wanted to
marry, and I had never felt that before. We wanted to
stay one more year in Africa, but there was a
presidential election coming up, and we wanted to be
back in the States for that. But this was a big time in my
life, going through all that and addressing the fact that
somebody I loved might die. And that I didn't have
anybody there to go through it with me. My mother and
father had no idea this was happening.

Both Erika and Marjorie were coming to realize that
the world is not an ideal place, that people who should have
been trustworthy could betray you. In a sense they lost their
innocence about the kind of place they expected their world
to be. They were going through a process of
disenchantment,[5] an important aspect of any rite of passage.
One effect of such experiences could be a loss of trust, an
unwillingness to try to understand others and to work with
them. Erika and Marjorie could have pulled back into
themselves and set tight limits on their world. On the other
hand, such experiences can help young people break out of

predictable expectations and limitations and to grow. Both Erika and Marjorie learned that they could survive painful experiences—not only survive, but be strengthened by them.

The battle with the beast is not once and for all. Confrontations with such ordeals will continue to challenge throughout life. But regression can occur anywhere along the journey when one chooses to step back into the prison of self-imposed limitations or peer expectations. However, if the lesson of the battle of the beast can be learned on the path from adolescence to adulthood on a conscious level, that lesson can be carried through life and reinforced each stage of the way. One must choose to be free from confining limitations and destructive expectations—and continue to choose all through life.

During the battle with the beast one becomes aware of inner resources that will never be called on unless pulled into an extreme situation. But one has to develop the ability to draw on those inner resources. Here is where skills in reflection taught by the guardian spirit become so valuable. One's extremity opens up the opportunity to grow, but the skills must be there and used.

The Victory:

"Wow . . . I learned something."

Challenge: to master certain skills
necessary for the task undertaken,
skills in working with
material and human resources,
and skills in accessing one's inner resources.

I n many indigenous cultures the young woman is taught
by an elder woman the role and skills she will need to
function in her new status as a potential wife and
mother. The young man has the opportunity to prove his
courage and prowess as a hunter and warrior. Built into
these experiences of gender identity are opportunities to
reflect on one's role and one's value to the whole
community. The young woman and young man prove to
themselves and to their village that they are worthy of
entering adulthood.

In the contemporary world the victory achieved
through the battle with the beast is a knowledge that one is
neither limited by self-perception nor peer-imposed
expectations, that one can endure in the face of a crisis
situation, and that one needs to develop both masculine and
feminine qualities to function effectively in the world, to be
a complete and balanced adult.

Barbara, during her two years with the Jesuit
Volunteer Corps, confirmed what she had always believed
about qualities that make a person a full human being:

I've always thought there are feminine qualities and there are masculine qualities, but those qualities don't necessarily go with women or men. I'm not sure where I got this idea, and I haven't found a lot of people who agree with me. I think the fact that I grew up in a house with all women [three sisters and our mother], except for my dad, made a big difference because I saw—for example—we all played sports. We all participated in feminine and masculine things.

I guess no one was going to tell me that this was my role, the feminine role. I'm very much a woman, but I guess, emotionally, I'm kind of on the masculine side because I'm not always that great at expressing myself. I think that's kind of more a masculine thing. But, again, that doesn't mean that that necessarily has to go with being a man.

During my year in Dallas, the men in our community— in terms of cooking and cleaning up—they were the hardest to get moving. The men and I struggled at first, because I went into it thinking, OK, don't try to give me this hogwash that you're a man, and you're going to have problems living in community because you're living with people who are women. We had a chore schedule. But in those situations when we had a party, we were all expected to chip in and help. Their [the men's] thing was, "Well, that's not my chore." And we [the women] said, "Well, that's not one of our chores either and we're doing it."

I was on the [house-keeping] team with the two men, which was very difficult . . . and we were cleaning the house and one of them wanted to mow the lawn. He thought that was part of cleaning the house. And I said, "No, that's not. We have this whole house to clean." There was definitely a difference of opinion.

Looking back now, I think that they came along quite a bit. But I also came along too: in accepting them, in finding ways to make things clearer, and in giving them more guidance on what needed to be done.

A turning point comes when the young person can perform the task somewhat automatically, when the work is no longer a great effort because the skills and the habits necessary for the work have been mastered and assimilated. There is no longer the panic that comes with the thought, "I don't know how to do this!" For both Erika in Costa Rica and Nate in Bangladesh, the language barrier was a formidable factor. Because Erika was in Costa Rica only three months with her college service program, she never quite broke through the language barrier, but she did penetrate her own psychological barrier, which was perhaps more important. Erika recalls:

> When you're in a place as different as Costa Rica was from my own American life, you're not comfortable. Everything gets stripped down, and you're just kind of naked. If these kinds of issues came up during orientation, I don't remember it 'cause I have a feeling that if they had said it, I wouldn't have heard it then. I don't think there's any way you can really tell someone it's going to be the toughest thing of your life, and they'll actually hear it. I think it's something you just live through. I don't know . . . it might be helpful to hear it. I don't know how I would have reacted.

> But I did stay there. I did deal with the language. I did function in spite of inadequate support. What helped me do it? I think it was people like . . . oh, can I remember her name? I think it was Cristina. She was 11 years old, I think, something like 11 or 12. And she would always come looking for me—she was one of the refugees—and grab my hand. We would go to their

home. It was just a shack with dirt floors. I'd never seen people live quite so poorly. And her mother, she would make these wonderful sweet rolls. They kind of reminded me of my mom's. And they bake them in this stone oven—you know, the kind that's rounded . . . oh, they were wonderful . . . and she had us over for breakfast one time, another student and me.

Cristina's mother must have had eight or nine kids, all running around, anywhere from twelve, which is Cristina's age, all the way down. And she set out the table and said, "We'll put on a tablecloth," and then served us eggs—scrambled eggs—which was quite a sacrifice. I know that because I was helping hand out food, and they don't get very much—especially eggs, which are pretty precious. And just the two of us ate and nobody else did. It was just their kindness, their generosity, despite not having anything. How could I even complain—and lack strength and courage—when I was seeing that? That really fed me on a deeper level, just the way the people were so beautiful, despite all the hardships and not being able to communicate all that well. I mean, that kind of a message comes through despite the language.

Nate recalls that he was around three months in-country when he experienced his own break-through in Bangladesh:

After about 90 days or so you begin to adapt. And all of a sudden the things that were so traumatic begin to be things of interest, things of challenge, things to get to know. And what was fear and trepidation turns into excitement and adventure. But it takes some time.

Look what Nate and Erika would have missed had they given up and gone home before the turn-around came.

There is another critical break-through: After a certain period of time, depending on the task, the young person gains a command of the resources, both material and human. He or she knows where to go for help, what materials to use, how to get hold of them, how to care for them, and sometimes how to multiply them. And finally, the emerging adult discovers not only is it possible but it is necessary to develop both masculine and feminine qualities to operate responsibly and compassionately in the world.

The ideal task for the full personal and spiritual development of the young person is one that demands both courage and initiative as well as sensitivity and compassion. The more that young people can develop these qualities within themselves, the less inclined they will be to make unhealthy demands on others to satisfy those needs. And, finally, their refined skills of reflection will provide the insights necessary to support their new level of understanding. These are the kinds of experiences which will eventually lead them to say, "Wow . . . I learned something!"

* * *

Chapter Six

Incorporation:
"Something happened."

T he young people who have separated from their
childhood, who have been willing to pay the price of
their departure, who have taken on the task, fought
the beast of perceived limitation, and won the victory of
insight and knowledge, are now ready to return and to be
incorporated into the community as transformed human
beings. They left their home adolescents and returned, if not
quite adults, at least well on their way to becoming so. In
other words, something happened to them along the way.

Traditional villages welcomed their young adults
back into the community with feasting and ceremony. The
village witnessed the fact that something significant had
happened, and they celebrated the transformation.

In contemporary urban culture there often is no
community to witness and celebrate—and thus validate—
the achievements of youth. Young people go off to test
themselves and return with no acknowledgment of what
they have accomplished.[1]

Without the validation of the act, the power of the experience dissipates. Or worse—as the experience of Vietnam veterans shows—the ordeal can lead to destructive behavior. Many came out of Vietnam afflicted with perpetual immaturity for a variety of complex reasons. This is not the place to go into them. However, one thing is evident: Because of the unpopularity of the war, the veterans' military experience was never validated; their "battle with the beast" never led to insight and victory; their return to the community was never celebrated.[2]

Tribal wisdom recognized the importance of bringing the journey to closure and celebrating the new status of the young adult. The insights and competencies gained during the journey must be acknowledged and celebrated. That very process reinforces them. Too frequently, unacknowledged and uncelebrated, human victories can be denigrated by the very youth who achieved them. When that happens the victories recede from memory and therefore from reality. Young people often don't realize what they have accomplished because the adult world has not noticed and celebrated with them.

The Return: *"I feel different."*

Challenge: to return to the community
a transformed person
willing
to share the new skills and insights.

There are two major questions at the time of the return: How does a service experience bridge the transition from the corps to the world? And how has the young person been transformed?

An ideal service experience will have four characteristics with respect to bringing the youth's term to a close: There should be some specific closure event, a celebration by the community, opportunities for sharing the fruit of the experience, and some kind of post-service career and personal benefits.

Jim remembers his passage from the Civilian Conservation Corps back into the world prior to World War II. There was no specific closure event nor celebration. There was, however, a post-service benefit, indirect as it was. And the rest of his life provided opportunities for sharing the fruit of his experience. He recalls,

> I was working on the Schran compressor up on the Gunflint Trail when I got my break to go to college. Now remember, this is the Depression, and nothing in my background ever led me to believe that I would go to college some day.
>
> Anyway, the Gunflint Trail was an avenue for people to come up to these beautiful lakes. Tourists at that time would come up to fish and would stay at the lodges or tent or whatever. And it was wild land, really wild. So what we would do, we would block everybody that came up. We had to block 'em 'cause if we were going to dynamite, they would have to wait there half an hour or an hour.
>
> One of the tourists that came up was the treasurer of Hamlin University. We stopped them—like I said—and then we talked. It was a way to kill time. He talked to me there on the trail. Then that night, a bunch of guys from camp wanted to go to a lake that was about 10

miles up from our camp and swim, and they didn't have a convoy driver. The regular one wasn't available or wouldn't drive 'em up. Because I still had a convoy permit, I volunteered to drive. And when I got up there, here was the treasurer and his wife out on the dock. Somehow or other, I impressed him.

So he asks me, he says, "What's a young guy like you doing up here in this sort of place?"

And I say, "Well, what's a young guy like me going to do? Out west the dust is blowing. There's nothin' there, just plain nothin'."

"You could go to college," he says.

"With what?"

"Well, apply."

So he urges me to apply to Hamlin University. Two weeks later I get a letter back from the director of admissions that tells me I don't have a chance. In the first place, he tells me, your high school exam record is very poor. What's more, you have no money.

Well, okay, I say, forget it. And I go back to working with the compressor. Then I get a letter, oh, about a week or so later from the director of admissions who says that the treasurer got back and asked the director of admissions, "Did you get a letter from that young guy I saw up there in the woods?"

"Yes, I did, and I told him he doesn't have a chance."

"Well, I tell you what, you write him again and tell him you would like to see him. Just get him down here, and you take a look at him."

Well then I had to get out of CCCs. You couldn't get out
unless you had a job. And my mother didn't want me out
'cause the money was just too much support to let go.
Twenty-five bucks was a lot of money. My father was a
horse-trader and a very poor provider. My Jewish uncle
who had married my Irish aunt—he was a bartender in
Minneapolis—well, when my mother said I didn't have a
job and couldn't get out, he wrote and said I had a job as
a chauffeur. That got me out of the CCCs. Then I went
down to the university. The director of admissions
talked to me for about two hours.

"You know," he tells me, "I think you can make it."

And I went out into the harvest fields and worked for 30
days, two bucks a day, made $60. Then my mother let
me have the last 25 bucks. Another kid and I hitch-hiked
to Hamlin. The director of admissions put us up in a co-
op. Twenty-eight guys lived in this building. It wasn't
heated up where we slept, so you can imagine how cold
we were in the winter.

Anyway, I started school. I made the freshman football
team immediately. At the end of the first semester, I was
on the honor-roll. I played basketball and was all-
Minnesota Conference my freshman year. I had a try-out
at the New York Yankees as a catcher that summer.
Didn't make it. That was the year Yogi Berra was
brought on the team. I went back to college as a coach
my sophomore year. My path was decided.

For Jim, service in the CCC opened up a path in life
he never could have imagined for himself. In fact, it was
because he was willing to "go the extra mile," literally, in
driving his buddies up to the lake as a favor, that he again
encountered the university treasurer whom he had met on
the trail earlier in the day and who would become a mentor

153

for him. Jim in time earned bachelors and masters degrees in physical education and science. He spent the next 50 years as a high school teacher of science and coach in three sports: football, basketball, and baseball.

Nate faced different challenges in coming home from Bangladesh in 1965. The world of the mid-'60s differed from the world of the mid-'30s in significant ways. And Jim and Nate came from different backgrounds and went into their service experiences with very different expectations. Nate remembers,

> As it got to be time to leave, the school where I taught had a good-bye celebration. The Peace Corps brought us all to Dacca, the capital, for a conference where we discussed our experience. The Peace Corps was trying to learn so they could do a better job. And we poured our hearts out. The one issue that sticks in my mind—it's funny what you remember—is that they didn't tell us how to take care of our underwear and how to deal with jock itch. So that went on the agenda. But there were other things about assignments and language training and so forth. We were in Dacca not more than a week. The closing-out conference was maybe three to five days. They gave us our tickets and our money to go home. Then we left.

For Jim and Nate there were some similarities: Both had gone to remote areas; both dealt with other cultures, and both faced a kind of shock when they came out. Nate calls it his reverse culture shock:

> Most people are glad to have you back. They want to know what you did. But you start to tell them and their eyes glaze over. Then you find yourself drifting toward people who have been in the same country or had other experiences where you have some commonality.

Nate realized that his perspective on life had changed considerably. He had re-framed his world:

> Now you have a broader lens on the world and your interests are broader. Yes, you're thinking about career, and you're thinking about the United States, but you're thinking about all that in terms of this perspective called "this earth and the world we live in." That remote place over there may seem insignificant from over here. But you've been in a place like that, and you know it's not insignificant to the people there. Truly, for all of us on this earth, it's not insignificant. What happens there affects us in some way. We've got to have a broader scope.

> When you come from a culture like ours, it's hard not to feel you are better because we have so much material wealth. It's hard not to fly into somebody's country who has nothing and to feel superior. But if you go in and live at the level of the ordinary people, you soon come to realize that these people have a culture that's been around longer than ours.

> The way they do things makes an awful lot of sense. Why not borrow from them as well as they borrow from us? I came to appreciate the unselfishness, the humanity, the honesty, the integrity, I saw in the people I worked with; whereas so much of what happens here is based on profit, selfishness, and commercialism.

> Now, there are good points about competition. I didn't come back thinking this is the worst place to be. I came back appreciating a lot about the U.S. But I also recognize there are lots of good things out there that could make this place even better.

Lessons. For instance, I was very used to our democratic way of life. You put a motion on the floor at a meeting; you debate it, and you vote on it. I don't remember the issue now, but at our faculty meetings we had gone round and round, debating it—no agreement among the staff—so I raised my hand and said, "Why don't we vote on it?" Someone said, "Voting divides." We just went on debating . . . but gradually a consensus emerged. No one had to back down. No one had to be on the wrong side of the issue. This lesson helped me later on back here, as a matter of fact, even working in my church. Sometimes bringing something to a straight vote right off the bat isn't the way to go.

I know I didn't realize how much all this would affect me when I started out. When I went over, I thought the effect would be bigger there. In all honesty, the effect was bigger on me, the impact on me rather than the impact I had there.

One of the things about being in a different culture is that it causes you to stop and think about what is really going on. What is the basis for humanity? I was in a culture so different and yet on a one-to-one basis I developed some wonderful, lasting friendships. There is something that transcends the cultural limitations, the language, the religion, and all that, which I won't say I fully understood at the time—but I began to see inklings.

This experience changed me to be more open, more willing to try things, more looking forward to doing something new and different. And all that brought me through. Spending two years in a culture that's been around for centuries, that started millennia before your own country did, and feeling like you're having almost no impact, was very humbling.

Impact. I did manage while I was there to teach some classes and I was able to build a science lab, which when I left I was afraid would never be used. I felt fortunate to go back there five years later and to see the lab. It was in such disarray and in bad shape from being over-used that I was jubilant. The problem is that it is so difficult to get a good piece of equipment that when they do, they lock it up and don't use it. So I was afraid when I left that they would lock up that science lab and show it to visiting dignitaries. But I could see that it had been used and practically destroyed from use. It really made me feel that my two years had accomplished something.

I, in turn, became a much more tolerant person. I'm now aware you can't judge something by the way it looks. I mentioned the way the men dressed, the way they held hands. I soon learned that those guys are just as much a man as I am. Even if something is totally different, it doesn't mean it's wrong or invalid or something that should be despised. If you open your eyes you're going to learn something. There are other ways of doing things. You learn when you encounter a challenge not to get stuck in one way of looking at it.

While it was tough getting started, I've never regretted my time with the Peace Corps. If I had to do it all over again, I would. I might be farther ahead financially if I hadn't spent that time as a volunteer, but I would not have given it up. It was the most interesting time of my life.

Returned Volunteers as Resources

When Nate returned to the States, he received a National Defense Fellowship for a large eastern university to continue studies in Bengali, which was one of the esoteric languages funded by the government. During the summers he helped train volunteers to go abroad at the University of Wisconsin. He also was offered a position to go to Laos:

> If I hadn't been accepted for the fellowship, I probably would have gone. It was all part of a Southeast Asian effort. I was single. They were looking for guys who would go because it was somewhat dangerous. I was interested. Sometimes I look back and think, gee, I wonder what would have happened if I had gone. It is evident that I got the fellowship because of my Peace Corps experience. It has shaped my life and career. It has given me skills and a level of patience and tolerance that I might not have learned as quickly otherwise. Those interpersonal skills are invaluable.

> I went to Afghanistan on Peace Corps staff. Then I worked on a U.S. AID (Agency for International Development) contract and ran the Fulbright Commission. So I did three things while in Afghanistan. I was there for eight years and met my future wife there. She was working for AID. After we were married, we went to Africa together and served with Save the Children after our first son was born. We probably would have stayed longer, but it wasn't the best situation for raising young children. We've been back in the U.S. now for 12 years.

Nate talks about his concern:

> I have stayed in the international field and have had input. But I could have done more if the government had said, "Hey, we spent X thousands of dollars on the education of those individuals [referring to his fellowship]; let's make sure they're doing some good." Where I am now, I got hired in the position because we started to do more with Pakistan and Egypt and Turkey.

Since I had expertise in that area, I was a natural. But it was more like tripping into it. It wasn't like the government saying, "Let's see if this guy is interested." Our government fails to tap the expertise of people like myself as well as they could. What a waste of a resource!

Another valuable resource is Paul, a Lutheran Volunteer Corps alumnus who worked with the urban homeless. He had earned his Masters degree from the John F. Kennedy School of Government and planned to take a law degree at Columbia following his term of service. He reflects on what he hoped to contribute:

> I realize that in one year [his term of service with LVC] you're not going to have much impact on your surroundings, but the major impact is what that experience is going to have on oneself. The hope is that when any of us is in a position where we can affect public policy we can bring these experiences to bear on our understanding and decisions.
>
> I felt as I was studying public policy at the Kennedy that I was getting a good analytic education. I was getting a sense of what the problems were from a theoretical point of view, but I didn't feel like I understood the problems from a personal perspective. I felt if I wanted to get into understanding and making policy, I should have a more direct, service-level experience. I think it's easy to forget that policies affect individual people. I thought this would be an experience that would really inform my professional life in the years to come.
>
> The catalog of the Kennedy School says that they are hesitant to grant deferments. So I didn't feel like that was an option. Looking back on it now, I think I could have talked to the dean and could have gotten a deferment. Maybe they are trying to deal with the

159

number of people who want to work on election campaigns. There are a lot more applicants in off-election years. On the other hand, Columbia Law School was very supportive of my deferment.

A growing number of colleges and graduate schools are realizing the value of deferment for the sake of granting an applicant time to gain some practical world experience to enrich the future classroom experience. Fred Hargadon, dean of admissions presently at Princeton and formerly at Stanford, has said as much to parents of pre-college students. He wishes there were a socially-acceptable way to get young people out of their academic straitjackets for a period of time before or during their college career, preferably a service experience, but if not that, some other positive experience.[3]

This is what Bill did. He went to City Year following his graduation from high school and was granted a deferment from his college of choice. His year of service gave him some "breathing room" as he thought about what he wanted to do with his life. His closure of the City Year experience was a "graduation." While many other young people lack public recognition for what they have accomplished, Bill felt there was almost too much attention paid to his City Year class that year. It was a media event, he recalls . . . but then he realizes the importance of media exposure for fund-raising.

Martin, two years out of college, remembers his own closure in 1961 in Jordan where he went to teach English. He had come under the Point Four Program, part of the Marshall Plan instituted by Truman in 1949. Martin's task was to teach Jordanian English teachers. His memory of its conclusion still brings a chuckle:

This was a kind of graduation celebration at the end of our six-week term. The 30 young men I had worked with had learned at some point in their program the song, "Old Macdonald's Farm." We had gone to a nearby park, and they asked me to lead them in the song. So I am leading. They are singing . . . and clucking and oinking and quacking . . . many of them off-key. Amidst all this ruckus, a man comes through the park with his wife and children. Hearing this terrible racket—and probably thinking, what are you doing creating this alien noise?—he comes up and gives me a shove, an invitation to fight if ever there was one. Fortunately, the students intervened. They were very embarrassed—but they sure loved that song.

Emily's experience was quite different. She had entered the Lutheran Volunteer Corps immediately after her graduation from college in 1991. The following year was a low-key closure experience in the LVC:

Our final retreat was in July. That was pretty much just a recreational thing. We camped out in tents. Not all of the volunteers came. It was an optional thing. There was no stated, "This is a celebration of our past year and a farewell kind of thing." On our own we would talk about what we were doing as we were hiking through the woods with volunteers we knew from other cities. A month later we finished the LVC year, about the middle of August.

Effect on Personal Life

Emily later became aware of the impact of the experience on her personal life. She completed her term with LVC but continued to work with the homeless at the agency, where she was hired full-time. She comments:

For me, the biggest change in leaving the Lutheran Volunteer Corps was leaving my community members. That was difficult. Maybe it was a couple of months later, I noticed the difference in my life style since I wasn't in intentional community. I was living with friends from college, friends who did not have anything like this kind of experience in a community where we would be intentional about planning and spending time together. I noticed that I had more time to myself after I left the community. I had more time to do things I wanted to do.

Probably for a year it was pretty comfortable, but in the second year I noticed something was missing from my life. I think it was what came from intentional community where my housemates were really supportive and we spent time together and shared each other's lives. We knew we were supportive of each other even when we weren't together.

For those corps members who live in community, saying good-bye becomes a more serious issue than for those who don't. Barbara, who spent two years with the Jesuit Volunteer Corps, the first year in Boston, the second in Dallas, remembers her "coming out." The JVC calls it "dis-orientation," the flip side, one might say, of orientation.

Dis-orientation in my second year was a very social thing—which was fine because at that point we just wanted to say our good-byes to each other. We had dis-orientation and then we went back to our [JVC] cities and worked for another month, so the year wasn't fully over yet. Now that's how the South [JVC region] does it.

In the East you have dis-orientation and you are done. I like it the way the South does because having dis-orientation at the end, it's too hard to say good-bye to everyone in the region and your community. It's just too rushed. So, this way it allowed us to say good-bye to the people in the region.

At dis-orientation they provided us with a lot of tips on what to do and what not to do when you're saying good-bye. That helped us out a lot because it made us say, OK, you only have a month left . . . you might be happy there is only a month left . . . but you want to make it the best. You don't want to totally ignore you're leaving and then zoom off or you're going to be unhappy. Well, it's going to be hard anyway.

But they gave us tips: like throw yourself a party so you can say good-bye to everybody. Have the community tell each person what they mean to you, and how much you're going to miss them. At the end, it was somewhat sad, but I guess for me when I'm leaving a situation I'm very much in denial. I even shake myself. I say, "You are leaving. Deal with it. Deal with it."

I deal with it physically . . . I say good-bye to people . . . but mentally it's so hard to grasp that concept. We had come to know people pretty well in the region. It was hard to say good-bye to them. But that last month in the community, that definitely helped us.

We did have a going-away party for ourselves. We had a meeting where we told each other how we thought about each other. The parents of one of our housemates gave us $50 to go out to dinner. So we took the steps necessary to say good-bye to each other.

Saying good-bye to colleagues and friends is only half of the process of "the return." Going home is the other half. Barbara remembers what happened to her:

I had a job in Washington which I had gotten over the phone, so I was going to go directly there. But even though I was 23 [years old], my mom said, "No, I want you to come home."

I hadn't been home since February, and my parents' thinking was, Come home for a few weeks and we'll provide for you. Just come home and relax for a little while.

There was definitely a change. My first year in Boston I was about six hours away from [my home in] Rochester, but I went home quite a bit. Whereas in Dallas I didn't go home that often, and it was the first time I had been away for a long time and been very happy and kinda not needed home. There was a big transformation there. Coming home—I was very excited to come home—but I realized I really can do this on my own now.

I didn't get homesick during the long time I was away. I was able to set out my own life. My parents had a hard time understanding that JVC had now become a full part of me . . . a lot of the values I was taking away with me. I think they thought, All right, you did that. Now let's move on.

For instance, when I was looking for a place to live, I was kind of looking for community, several other people. And I remember my father said, "You're not in JVC anymore. You can't have that situation, so stop looking for it." And that's not true. There are community houses.

Barbara did find community in Washington, D.C., where she worked for several years before going on to graduate school.

Suzanna, who was in the Brethren Volunteer Corps in 1981-82 in Vermont, reflects on her closure:

> We had decided as a group at orientation to have a newsletter and we would all write letters. Greta (my partner in BVC) and I were elected to be the newsletter editors. So we'd receive all these wonderful letters and type them up. Our site sponsor allowed us to use the office equipment there to reproduce and send out the newsletters. So Greta [the corps member from Germany who lived and worked with me] and I did this final newsletter, which was one way of saying good-bye—and here's where we're all going to be.
>
> And in the church that sponsored us, I know there was something [to say good-bye], but I can't remember what. In the housing complex [where we had lived and worked during the year], the mothers' group had a little party for us. They gave us matching coffee mugs because we had always come together to drink coffee or tea.
>
> Many times I think, if I had known then what I know now, I would love the chance to go back and do things a little differently, to try to enable the residents of the complex to make the changes they wanted for themselves, instead of our being the catalyst for everything that happened.
>
> I think this experience made a huge difference to me because it made real to me things I read about in the newspaper, the whole thing that happens among low-income people, the struggles they have. When I found out I was going to a public housing project, I got all kinds of images of run-down tenement buildings, and I was really surprised to pull up to this pretty nice modern apartment complex, but that didn't mean that it was problem-free inside.

Alcoholism was a major problem there. It was the first time I ever met anybody who was an alcoholic. I didn't know anything about alcoholism and drug abuse and violence, but you can bet I learned pretty fast. A couple of times I saw some things that were really distressing.

And also there was the stigma that was attached to being in public housing. Greta and I both felt that. We'd take our film to the K-Mart to be processed and would have to list our address as being in Meadowbrook. Maybe we were too sensitive, but [the stigma] seemed real.

The experience opened my eyes to something I hadn't known anything about. Not just that, but my eyes were also opened to social issues. You know, in the early '80s, concern about nuclear weapons was tremendous. I'm not sure, if I'd stayed [home] in Tucson, the people that I worked with and hung out with . . . those weren't concerns of theirs. It wasn't anything we ever discussed. It's hard for me to imagine what the world was that I lived in, but it was kind of Tupperware parties and bridal showers, stuff like that.

There was a time, a couple of years after that, that I felt so separated from my friends in Tucson because I didn't think we had anything in common. All these serious things were happening in the world, and it was never a part of our discussion or letters. When I went to visit, it was something that nobody was very interested in. One of my older relatives said at one point after I had moved across the state to work in a shelter, "When are you going to get a real job?"

That, to me, sort of summarized the attitude of the Tucson group, that it wasn't real work that I was doing. Or at least it wasn't very important. While I was working in the shelter, I went with members of the church and the community to protest at Groton,

Connecticut against the launching of the nuclear submarines, and to New York in 1982 for another protest. I know from my dad it was scary to him for me to be involved in those things. I was doing it through my church, and he didn't know anything about the church. He wasn't a church-goer at all. Now I can understand better why he was concerned.

Suzanna never returned to the world of Tupperware and bridal showers. She remained in Vermont and continued to work on urban social issues and later took her hard-won expertise to Washington, D.C.

Marjorie reflects on her culture shock on finishing her Peace Corps term in Togo and returning to the United States:

There was the physical thing. For two years I wore nothing but those rubber flip-flops. It was a shock to have to go back to real shoes. But there was also the mental thing. My students were convinced that the whole thing about an astronaut being on the moon was a hoax, that it had never happened. It was impossible, and it was just American propaganda. This country ceased to exist for me after I had been in Africa for about a year. I could not believe that there was a place like the United States of America.

Marjorie also remembers how much her thinking was altered during her experience in Togo:

It was in Africa that I became conscious of being grown up. For me it was living in my own house, making my own decisions, and nobody in my family even knew where I was at that moment. I could be doing something, and I would think, nobody I know has any idea that I'm at this spot doing this thing right now. It didn't happen right away. I'd say it was a year before I thought that way.

I was teaching 7th through 10th grade, English as a foreign language. What I got out of it was far more than what I gave to the country. I went with a lot of idealistic thoughts, but it was much more my experience than that I did anything great for the Togolese. I gained a whole different perspective on life—totally different—that has affected every day of my life since I lived there. I came out of it with a different set of priorities than I had gone in with. It's almost like putting on a different pair of lenses, seeing the world from a different point of view than I had before I went.

If I were to go into the Peace Corps again, I think I could go more as a giver now. I think then just coming out of college I was more of a taker. The people around me wouldn't say that because I worked hard at my job. I was a good teacher, but there were a lot of things I didn't notice. There were questions I didn't ask, a lot of things I might have been able to do if I hadn't been so wrapped up in myself. I was very wrapped up in myself for the two years I was there . . . learning to cope with solitude, spending a lot of time alone . . . thinking a lot and writing a lot and reading a lot and growing up a lot.

I went to a country where the most important things in life are family and friends, and where the consumer society just doesn't exist. I didn't understand what the consumer society was until I lived in a society that wasn't. And I'm a real lover of the United States. I knew I couldn't live in West Africa for the rest of my life. I knew I had to come back here. I just love the U.S., but I know I see it more for what it really is now. In my own life my priorities are different than if I had not had this experience. I wouldn't have had children as early as I did. I wouldn't have married as young as I did.

I might not have had the courage to be an educator instead of being the wife of a rich doctor.

Marjorie's husband Steve, who had been so appalled at what he perceived as the backwardness of the people, adds,

When you live over in Africa you get a whole new idea of the difference between what you need and what you want. When you live in America, it's a 24-hour-a-day bombardment of "You need all these things." When you get over to Africa, you don't need any of them. All you need is some water, some rice and beans, and a shirt to wear. In America you're convinced that you need a whole lot more.

The whole concept of family . . . families living closely together, relying on each other for everything. I came back and I didn't have to be a stockbroker or a lawyer. After two months, though, I did have to have a microwave, I'll tell you that. It didn't take long to get reprogrammed. At least you're conscious of the fact that you've been reprogrammed. You can always remind yourself, "Well, I don't really need the microwave." . . . except I really did need it. I had to have it!

The service experience in Africa had re-framed the world for Marjorie and Steve. They married when they returned to the United States. Over the next ten years they became parents to two boys and dedicated themselves to the teaching profession. And, yes, Steve did get his microwave.

Ron, who spent his teenage years during the 1980s as a Red Cross volunteer, both as a recreational assistant at a school for the blind every week and as a swimming instructor, came to appreciate what the American Red Cross contributed to his growing up. For three summers during his high school years he attended the Red Cross Leadership Development Center in his home state. The summer following his graduation from high school he was selected by the Red Cross as an American delegate to the international conference of youth held in Austria that year. During his month there he met delegates from all over the world. He remembers:

> I saw youth delegates from Israel and Egypt come together in Austria, bonded together by a humanitarian cause that went beyond their political issues. And I met Hungarians there—they were still part of the Eastern Block then—and came to realize that people in communist countries don't hate us. I discovered they love life as much as I do. They were just as curious about us as we were about them.
>
> The big shock came when I returned to the U.S. I was scheduled to go into a Navy ROTC at my new college. Right after my return I had to go to indoctrination, which is like the Navy boot camp. We had a gunnery sergeant yelling at us stuff like, "Kill a commie for mommy." I just couldn't deal with that. As I was holding my rifle at attention, and the sergeant was calling me an idiot, I was thinking, There's got to be a better way to deal with the world than this.

After a year Ron reevaluated what he wanted to do with his life and left the NROTC. Following graduation he sought a grant which enabled him to intern with the Red Cross National Headquarters in Washington, D.C. for a year. During that time he spent a month with a disaster team in Puerto Rico. That was the year Puerto Rico was hit with both hurricane Hugo and an earthquake. Ron could speak functional Spanish and spent his time delivering supplies with a Spanish-speaking partner.

These kinds of experiences made Ron realize how much the Red Cross believes in young people through their youth programs. He recalls something a friend once said:

> "If you treat somebody the way they *should* be, then they can become what they ought to be." That's what the Red Cross did for me. Too bad more kids don't know about its youth programs.

Emerging into Adulthood

Tom, who graduated from college in 1990, hoped to go into teaching. He was not sure at that point at what level or exactly where, but he knew he wanted to reach people and to be taken seriously. He comments,

> I felt like I needed to have experience and not just a text book approach. So I set out from college and gave myself two years—it's been three years now—to do as many different things as I could that would give me a range of experiences. I wanted to be able to say, yes, I have worked with this population of kids. Yes, I have done the environmental thing . Yes, I have worked in the city. Now I can speak from some base of knowledge.

A college term in Mexico gave him experience working with refugees. The summer following graduation he was a counselor for six weeks with severely disturbed children, which to this day he says was the most difficult challenge he ever confronted. Then he spent four months with Jubilee Partners, an ecumenical Christian-based organization in Georgia, working with Central American refugees. From January until June he was an intern with an outdoor environmental camp in New Hampshire. During this time he was doing some hard thinking about the direction of his life. He recalls:

> When I got back from Mexico, I was so convinced that I needed to go back and work with Mexican refugees. Yet I was told in many direct and indirect ways that these same problems exist right in my own backyard. "Have you ever looked?" Well, no, I hadn't. I needed to, but it was going to be hard. I didn't want to go to a city, but I felt I had to get this kind of experience. So I imposed this on myself. I chose to come to an inner city where I would be a minority. Other than in Mexico, I had never lived where I was a minority.

Stimulated by the magazine, *Sojourners*, which challenged him to think about how he might use his life, he decided to spend a year with the Sojourners community in Washington, D.C. They had an opening for a VISTA, which Tom applied for and was accepted. He lived in the Sojourners community house and worked with a children's center. He was attracted to Sojourners because he saw them as people committed to living and working with the poor and basing their lives on their understanding of the gospel. If that's how they base their lives, he thought, I just have to go and be with them and learn.

As that term ended, he discovered Public Allies. Here was a program open to young people—18 to 30 years of age—providing them an opportunity to spend a year as interns with non-profits in urban areas. At the same time they could get training in leadership skills, conflict resolution, and community organizing. Tom was accepted into Public Allies in Washington where he spent his year's internship working with the Association for Renewal of Education (ARE). He was a liaison for the Youth Homes, temporary shelters for court-referred young people.

In reflecting on his three years since college, he knows that he is in a very different place than he was at the time of his graduation. But something haunts him:

> I'm sort of disappointed because I feel that as I learn
> more about the reality of the world, it makes me
> reconsider this idealism I had. Maybe I'm just getting
> more realistic. I realize now I can't change the world in
> my lifetime. I can only do a little piece here and there.
> Yet the change you hope for can't be just on the surface.
> It's got to be deep inside. For instance, I have to be
> really honest with myself. I realize that I still hold some
> unfair judgments. I don't always feel like I love people.
> I feel that for whatever reasons I'm just not effective yet.
> So I haven't yet come out the other end, but I have
> changed. I don't know whether I'll ever come out. It's
> one of those life questions.

Shortly after this reflection on his "disenchantment" process—a necessary part of his journey—Tom was accepted into graduate school. By that time he realized he wanted to teach high school. He felt ready to move more deliberately toward his goal—and ultimately toward adulthood.

Erika, who was with the Mennonite Volunteer Corps, reflects on her dawning awareness of being an adult:

> I can't say the day, but maybe the time period. It hasn't
> been all that long ago. I felt independent with my
> thinking for a long time, but now . . . now it's more my
> home is here in D.C. It's no longer in Iowa. I often say,
> I'm going to Iowa instead of I'm going home. I've had to
> consciously say that.
>
> It may be kind of a silly thing, but for me it's important
> to make that distinction. I think it has to do with having

a job that is not a one year kind of thing. Just feeling a little more permanent and a part of the community here, and that takes time. I've put that time into it and I'm feeling like putting some roots down. For me, D.C. is home now. It won't be forever. When I go to graduate school, I'll leave here. That's probably another five years off.

The women I work with here at the shelter are children. I'm 25 and I'm parenting a lot of the women here who are twice my age because they're like children . . . for a variety of reasons, some of it mental health stuff. For some, it's more than that, it's that they never grew up.

But Erika did grow up . . . and Steve and Marjorie and Tom and Barbara and Nate and the others who took their journeys out into the world and encountered their guardian spirits and fought their beasts and achieved their victories. They returned home transformed because of their discoveries: discoveries about the difference between needs and wants, about the value of relationships, about a true sense of humility in reflecting on their small contribution to the human experience, but also about their infinite worth as individuals, as contributors to the world community. They learned how to identify and to create resources and to make them available to others. They learned how to give and to share, not just to take. These are journeys that have changed their lives forever.

* * *

Part III. Right of Passage

Achieving Adulthood

So what is adulthood? How do we know when we've grown up? One thing is certain: Adulthood doesn't just happen. Nor is it signaled simply by rising consumption of stuff, as advertisers would have us believe.

Adulthood is not an assumption but an achievement. Traditional cultures have given their young the right of passage into adulthood through participation in rites of passage. Every culture provides benchmark experiences for stages of life as well as the perspective through which to view these stages. For instance, in Native American culture the young man is ready to enter manhood when he has sought and found his vision under the guidance and care of the elder men, the young woman her womanhood when she has had her first menses and separated from the village for her instruction by the older women. The whole village plays a role.

In contrast, our culture tells us our children have entered adolescence when they start buying designer jeans and acne ointment. A *New York Times Magazine* essay describes the benchmark of turning 13 in one girl's life:

getting pierced for a belly-button ring. As described by her father, the trauma, for both himself and his daughter, carried an almost mythic dimension.[1] In the inner-city the so-called life script of young women leads teenagers to produce babies long before adulthood because that is the benchmark for growing up.[2]

The language we use to describe an experience frames the way we perceive the experience. It tells us how to interpret events. Expressions like "He's just sowing his wild oats" as an excuse for promiscuity, or "My friends think something is wrong with me" as the lament of a 15-year-old who has yet to conceive a child, or "Marriage is just a piece of paper" as the reason to avoid public commitment, would all seem to say that community expectations can lead to destructive behavior. Some communities are working together to change the language as well as the thinking and acting.

One example is mothers who choose to shift the perspective on menstruation of their pubescent daughters from "the curse" to the entry to womanhood and plan rituals to celebrate the event. Another example is a New England community's preference for the label "character education" over "sex education." Called the "Loving Well" curriculum, it uses literature to explore moral decisions regarding sexuality.[3] Yet another example is the fatherhood movement with its effort to raise the awareness of male parenting as essential, rather than extraneous, to the development of their children.[4]

Research tells us that knowledge-based programs alone are not effective in deterring destructive behavior. Youngsters have to develop the skills—including more adequate vocabulary—to think about choices and the strategies to deal with them.[5] Consider the growing currency of such terms as "Squash it!" "responsible sex," "designated driver," "win-win," "waging peace," and, most recently, "Smoking isn't cool."

Because the viewpoints of one's family and community about an experience are as important as the experience itself, *both* the experience and the language used to frame it are critical. When a heavy-duty term like "rite of passage" is used as a description, the experience had better be substantial enough to bear the weight, or the metaphor will crumble like a cookie dunked in milk.

The use of "rite of passage" in our mass media as a throw-away term to describe destructive experiences as markers for growing up both trivializes the term and denigrates the process. If experiences such as smoking, drinking alcohol, doing drugs, going to prison, hitting the beaches during spring break, and teen-age pregnancy are put forth as "rites of passage," then cynicism about coming-of-age will be inevitable.

On the other hand, when examples of a "heroic journey"—whether it be a personal journey through a difficult life situation or a more public journey through something such as a youth corps experience—are held up as the way to go, the attitudes of the community at large will more likely empathize with and support young people making their way to adulthood.

So, how do we help adolescents find this path? Many paths are good and many are healthy, but regardless of which is chosen, the *right* of passage is critical: That is, every young person should *earn* the right of passage into adulthood. However, just as important: Adults must *support* the right of healthy passage into adulthood and provide appropriate ways to mark it. The survival of our society demands it.

Two issues are at stake here: One, how does a young person find an appropriate way to earn the right to adulthood? Two, how does a community provide opportunities for healthy passage?

Chapter Seven, from the viewpoint of the young person making the choice, and Chapter Eight, from the view of the policy makers, will deal respectively with the two questions, both through the prism of the "heroic journey." In addition, they both focus on youth service as an experience usually significant enough to transform young lives. Chapter Nine discusses, for those who have yet to choose, why some paths may be better than others.

Chapter Seven

The Journey Beckons:
Which Path Shall I Take?

How does a young person choose the path? Contemporary challenges complicate the question. Hence the value of a narrative approach such as the heroic journey because it provides a logic for considering the question. The resulting discussion is organized around the heroic journey touchstones: the call, departure, encounter with the guardian spirit, taking on the task, doing battle with the beast, victory, and the return.

The Call

How do you find out about service corps options?

High schools and colleges can play a major role here. The library and/or guidance counselor's office should devote adequate shelf space to up-to-date references to youth corps, but the youth corps must also be responsible for getting information out to appropriate channels.

Sharon, who decided to join VISTA in 1992, underwent a frustrating search for any kind of information on the organization at her large midwestern university. She worked in the university library and finally found old out-of-date catalogs with old telephone numbers. Finally, through telephone information, she was able to track down the current number and talk with the appropriate office in Washington, D.C. to start the process rolling. A less persistent person would have given up. Fortunately, VISTA has taken on new life under AmeriCorps and its supportive legislation.[1] Up-to-date catalogs and information are now available.

Naturally the religion-based corps can and do recruit through their churches and denominational high schools and colleges. In addition, many colleges now have volunteer fairs, both for part-time student-based community service as well as for full-time post-graduate service. Furthermore, a new industry is opening up: interim consultants. These individuals give young people an overview of a whole range of options, not just service, but also apprenticeship and internship programs. This route, however, can be a rather expensive way to go.[2]

When considering the many options, it is important for the young person and his/her parents to consider the following:

- Do you want a full-time or a part-time opportunity?

- Do you want an international or a domestic experience?

- Do you want a one-semester, or a one- or two-year term of service?

Full-time or Part-time? There is no question that a full-time experience has a more profound impact than part-time. The full-time experience, by its nature, is total immersion and demands that the corps member take on a new role. Research tells us that the new role is the most critical factor in the maturing process.[3]

There is, however, an option where service is part-time and combined with an academic program. It is structured in a way that removes students from their resident college and home and puts them into a new environment and therefore demands of them a new role. Examples of this option include the Learning through Serving of the Episcopal Colleges and the Partnership in Service-Learning as well as the Goshen College program.[4]

International or Domestic? The prime example of an international option is the Peace Corps. But many college programs, such as the Episcopal and Mennonite, offer international opportunities. VISTA is usually the prototypical example of the domestic option. But domestic alternatives have virtually exploded in the past decade, ranging from the new civilian conservation corps to the urban corps to the religion-based corps.

But whether international or domestic, the experience almost inevitably will be intercultural. The suburban youth going into the city, and the inner-city youth going into a conservation corps, both have an intercultural experience. It does happen, however, that urban youths join urban corps that work in or near their own neighborhoods. But, even here, their corps-mates often represent racial and ethnic diversity, and the experience can still become intercultural.

Length of time? College programs tend to be three to five months, the period of an academic term. This is long enough to open up a profound experience, as happened to Erika, who went to Costa Rica with her college program, but may be too short to make the kind of breakthroughs that usually take a minimum of three months and often longer. It frequently happens that just as the student is mastering the skills to work with some degree of facility and comfort, it is time to go home.

The typical time span for domestic programs is one year. VISTA and the religious or faith-based corps offer a year's term. The urban programs, such as City Year and the DC Service Corps are 10-month and 11-month programs respectively, following the academic calendar. Overseas programs are typically two years. Nate's and Joe's experiences in the Peace Corps show that it takes about a year to get through all the hurdles in working effectively in a completely different culture, especially where the language is radically different.

The Departure

What kind of sacrifices are you able and willing to make for the sake of responding to the call?

Most young people by the end of adolescence have had some experiences of separation from home and friends for a variety of reasons, from visits to relatives to high school field trips to going away to college. But the separation demanded by a service corps has a different tone because it should help terminate financial and emotional dependence on parents. Whether a service corps is residential or live-at-home, it is an entry into a new phase of life in a way that is different from other experiences. For that reason it is helpful to consider the following:

- Do you want a residential program where you must leave home to engage in your service or do you prefer to live at home and do your service on a daily basis?

- Would you prefer to live alone or in a community?

- Do you need or desire a living stipend or do you have the resources to support a tuition-based program?

Residential vs. Home-based? The old CCC, the Peace Corps, and the early VISTA all demanded that the corps member say good-bye to family and friends and set out for "uncharted" territory. A good part of the adventure was precisely that of moving out into the unknown. This carried with it an exhilaration as well as a terror, as some of the stories of corps members indicate. Young people bring very different considerations to such a choice. Some youth will not consider leaving their friends, no matter how appealing an adventure might be. Others will consider going only if at least one other friend comes with them.

One of the problems with college-based international service programs is that students who go together to another country sometimes stick together like glue, creating a kind of cultural bubble around themselves. They miss half of the experience because of their unwillingness to separate. On the other hand, some college students will deliberately choose an international program not offered by their own college precisely because they don't want to end up in their own college enclave merely moved to another country.

Many of the urban corps draw members from within their own cities. Examples are City Year, the DC Service Corps, and City Volunteer Corps of New York. Many of the members—and in Washington, D.C. and New York City, most of them—continue to live at home and to work sometimes within their own neighborhoods or nearby. We need research to determine what difference a program makes on those who leave their city and home and relocate compared with one whose members remain at home.

Some urban corps, however, especially those based on a City Year model, also draw a large proportion of their members from other locations.[5] But all diversify their teams of approximately 10 to 12 members in terms of age, race, background, and educational level. The very fact of working together brings the participants into a multicultural experience. Even though some of the members may be returning to their homes every evening, they are spending their days working with and sometimes serving other cultures.

Living Alone or in Community? A young person's temperament is often a clue to this choice. The kind of isolation of a Peace Corps assignment may be intolerable to young people who would otherwise have a strong desire and the personal qualities to contribute to a different kind of service experience. It's good to know that one does not have to choose isolation if going overseas. Faith-based corps provide the community experience and have a wide variety of service sites. In addition, the members of the faith-based communities are seldom of only one religion. In fact, some of the most provocative religious discussions arise out of sharing a community with those of other faiths.

Julie, a Catholic with the Jesuit Volunteer Corps, lived in a community including three non-Catholic women. At first she felt defensive and resisted their need to express their religious views. Eventually she realized their feelings were as legitimate as her own and grew to acknowledge and respect them. They, in turn, had chosen the Catholic organization because the JVC offered the kind of opportunities they desired in Alaska. Both sides gained by living together in the community.

On the other hand, living in community makes its own kinds of demands. The rewards are great: increased interpersonal skills and the resulting satisfaction of belonging to an extended "family." Yet it may not be easy to get along with these new "family members." In contrast, the Peace Corps too has its rewards and challenges: growing skills in dealing with solitude and in finding other sources of companionship. Yet the loneliness can be intense. Either way, growth is inevitable—if the corps member is open and willing to learn.

Living Stipend or Tuition-based? Most college graduates feel ready for, and many depend on, a self-sustaining program. In other words, their participation depends on earning a living stipend. To remove the stipend would make the experience available only to those young people wealthy enough to afford it. In some cases, it's not just a matter of family wealth, but youthful pride. The time has come, they say, when I must make it on my own. I no longer wish to be dependent on my parents. This kind of financial independence is important to the maturing process.

On the other hand, many students who are still in college choose to take advantage of a service-learning program, one that is parent-dependent, but one that is often open to college-aid or scholarship help. Such programs cost no more than tuition would be at the home campus, and some can cost considerably less, especially in developing nations, according to the Institute of International Education. Furthermore, there are sometimes possibilities for a college-based service-learning program to grant a modest stipend, depending on the number of hours of service a week and the length of the term of service.

Encounter with the Guardian Spirit

Has some sort of underlying vision for your life
started to emerge?

A question I used to ask my students was, "What lights
your fire?" The answer to that question was more important
to me than what their grades were when I wrote
recommendations for them. All young people, if not totally
deadened by life circumstances, get excited about
something. Finding that something is the object of any kind
of "vision quest." The guardian spirit experience, whether
it's a dream or vision for oneself, a spiritual insight within
one's religious practice or prayer, an orientation to a new
phase of life or a personal mentor, can support and guide
that quest. Most programs, during the admissions process,
ask for a personal essay explaining why you want to join the
corps.

A related question is how open are you, not only to
learning how to learn, but to learning how to be taught? A
conscious development of both skills can have a profound
impact on the rest of your life. Even in extreme situations,
research tells us the ability to reach out to and connect with
a significant adult can spell the difference between disaster
and survival for young people who are in high-risk
conditions.[6] Youth corps programs must take seriously the
training and professionalism of the staff members, the team
leaders, and the mentors. But the young person coming into
a program must have the willingness to be open to the
relationship. Public awareness is growing of the importance
of the quality of these kinds of relationships.[7]

Consider the following:

- Do you presently have a non-family member adult friend with whom you can talk freely?

- Have you checked on the types of orientation of your chosen program, its philosophy, and its mentors?

- Do you prefer a program with an initial orientation only or one with periodic retreats?

Non-family Adult Friend. The evidence is that relatively few adolescents have true adult friends.[8] Even teachers, given the press of their schedules, are able to spend little one-on-one time with their students. Our culture must adjust itself to make possible greater interaction between the generations. Age segregation is as insidious as race segregation, and the resulting loss to the human community is serious from both.

But one adult friend is not enough. As valuable as that one is, and to be appreciated and nurtured, it should be a stimulus to further intergenerational friendships. Each of these relationships develops additional facets of the human beings involved—on both sides of the relationship. Older people are as much in need of youthful relationships as young people of older relationships.[9] Going into a transition in one's life already fortified with such friendships can open the way for further "guardian spirit" experiences.

Orientations, Philosophy, and Mentors. Find out about the orientation: how long it is, where it takes place, how many people will be participating, what kinds of activities it will include, and perhaps most important, what kinds of reflective activities will be demonstrated and encouraged.

This is a period of life when enormous change will take place. It is critical to document that change by sharpening one's skills in keeping a journal, in carrying on focused discussions, and learning other reflection strategies, because such processes will expand the learning capability.

Often young corps members are not aware of the philosophy of the corps until they find themselves in the orientation. It would be better if they knew what they were walking into before they sign up. This is an important factor in deciding which corps to join. Nate became aware of the Peace Corps philosophy in 1963 when, during his orientation, he saw himself trained as a "Cold Warrior," to "win the hearts and minds of the third world." It was quite overt. And because he continued as a staff member, he also watched the Peace Corps philosophy evolve toward international development, humanitarian aid and assistance, and nation-building.

VISTA went through its own political evolution, from involving "the disadvantaged in the decision-making processes which affected their lives" during the 1960s to moving toward the professionally skilled volunteers—architects, doctors, and lawyers—during the 1970s to citizen participation and community self help during the 1980s to emphasis on education, environmental programs, human needs, and safety under AmeriCorps in the '90s.[10]

The religion-based corps share four tenets that infuse the lives of the corps-members with a special quality: the attempt to live a simple life style, concern for social justice, intentional community, and commitment to spirituality. Agreement to these four tenets demands of the corps members a conscious reflection on their attitudes and behavior, on the choices they make.

Mentoring opportunities should open up during the orientation. But it is critical to point out to the incoming corps members that not every staff member and/or team leader will be an ideal mentor for every corps member. There may be personality-conflicts or personality-misses that can't be helped. Not all adults have the sensitivity to avoid sarcasm or brusque remarks that turn off potential friendships. Strategies for dealing with the inevitabilities of the human condition should be dealt with openly and honestly.

If the parents and/or adult friends of the young corps members can talk about these issues with them before they leave for their service term, all the better. This can help inoculate the young person to a possible lack of adult mentoring at the site. When Carol and her fellow VISTA members in Montana discovered the staff member was inadequate as a mentor, Carol took on that role for her peers.

Furthermore, young people can discover their own mentors from the population they are serving, as Nate did in Bangladesh and Joe in India. Mentors—like gold—can be discovered in the most unexpected places. Somehow the young person has to open up to that possibility. This is what "learning how to be taught" means. Our teachers can arise under the most unusual circumstances, much like little Cristina and her mother did for Erika in Costa Rica.

Initial Orientation Only or Periodic Retreats?
As a VISTA volunteer I had a four-day orientation with 35 other volunteers. During that brief period of time I grew to appreciate the wide diversity of age, race, ethnicity, and socio-economic spectrum. I realized the enormous potential for mutual sharing and for becoming resources to each other. We all agreed there should be an opportunity for coming together some time before the end of our year's term. That did not happen. The reasons are too complex to go into here. Unfortunately, we all went to our respective

sites, got buried in our respective jobs, and very soon lost the kind of *esprit de corps* that identified us as VISTAs. My experience tells me that Peace Corps and VISTA are significantly different in this regard: the special sense of identity is very strong in Peace Corps, not so strong in VISTA.

An important feature in the faith-based corps is the periodic retreat, usually four a year, one each season. The corps members within a region come together for a three-day weekend. They gather at a camp or retreat center for a time of physical relaxation, reconnection, and sharing with fellow volunteers, and plenty of time for fun as well as for structured, planned activities.

Emily remembers especially her second retreat with the Lutheran Volunteer Corps where the theme was solitude. Time was available for the participants to immerse themselves in it, to write or read, to think about the importance of it in their lives. Another time they talked about discipline, all phases of discipline: self-discipline in regard to day-to-day work, the discipline of their spiritual lives, and the discipline of commitment to friends and family. Emily also remembers her fellow LVC members who were non-Lutheran sharing their religious beliefs at one of their retreats. Religious diversity is the expectation rather than the exception in all of the faith-based corps.

Taking on the Task

What kind of work do you want to be doing for the next year or two?

Your major in college may be a clue. People in English and education often go into teaching. People in the social sciences often work with housing, hunger, health, and other urban projects. People in environmental studies often go into the conservation corps. On the other hand, the corps experience also provides an opportunity for corps members to try their hand at something totally different from their experience in college.

There are several questions, however, to consider:

- Do you know you work better with a highly defined job description, or do you enjoy helping to create your task?

- What kinds of skills do you need for your new task, or what skills must you develop on the job?

- In what ways can your background experiences help you in the experience to come?

- Would you prefer to work in a team-based or a solo-based corps?

Highly Defined vs. Loosely Structured Job Description? In spite of the fact that many of the tasks in the early Peace Corps and VISTA programs were loosely structured—in some cases non-existent—and would appear to result from administrative sloppiness, the young people who were creative self-starters designed work that often was more appropriate and effective in the long run. This is not to suggest that job descriptions be deliberately vague, but it is to give credit to the ingenuity of young people and to draw on that ingenuity in the continual redesign of job programs. Each corps member brings unique skills and personality characteristics to a job. The corps should take advantage of these gifts and make them work for the program.

All that being said, the young people going into the experience should also be able to expect that the job description they have signed up for is pretty close to what they will actually be doing. Some kind of contact with corps alumni is helpful: letter exchange or, preferably, face-to-face interchange to get some first-hand advice. The interviews for this book indicated that those who were teaching usually faced fewer surprises in their job description than those doing other kinds of projects.

But it's good for each one of us to take a look at ourselves and discover whether we function better with highly defined work parameters, or if our "highs" come from creating our own role.

Skills Brought to the Job vs. Skills Learned on the Job? The question faced by Peace Corps from the beginning was whether to favor the generalists or those who were skill-specific. Skill-specific is winning out these days, which in turn raises the average age of Peace Corps volunteers. But with the present variety of corps, there is theoretically an opportunity for almost anyone who has a desire to serve and a willingness to learn on the job.

Language is a prime skill, both brought to the job—as was the case with Marjorie and Steve, who brought skills in French to their job in Togo—and learned for the job—as was the case of Nate who learned Bengali for his work in Bangladesh. Erika brought rudimentary Spanish skills to Costa Rica but recognized how much she still had to learn to function effectively. The Mormon experience shows how the cultural expectation of service in the missions can help build an extraordinary language program at Brigham Young University.[11]

Most of the corps assign the corps member to jobs they will remain with for the duration of their service. The urban corps, in contrast, provide corps members with a range of experiences: physical labor, such as rebuilding inner-city parks and cleaning up river fronts; urban services, such as helping the homeless and working in food pantries; and education, such as tutoring in classrooms and after-school programs. Both options have advantages: Staying with one job for the full term gives the time and opportunity to attain some mastery, while the diversity of experiences gives young people an opportunity to try their hand at a variety of projects, to see what they like and are good at and might like to focus on in the future.

The urban corps, with their variety of experiences, would seem to be more suitable to younger corps members, and indeed that is the case. The urban corps invite participants from age 17 to 23; whereas Peace Corps and the religion-based corps have a base age of 21 and no upper age limit. This is as it should be; the latter corps, by their nature, require greater maturity. Nate remembers when Peace Corps in the early days was taking young people right out of high school—there were three or four of them in Bangladesh with him—but had to stop recruiting that age because the volunteers weren't mature enough for the demands of working, often alone, in developing nations.

Background Experiences?   The kinds of skills brought to the job can range from plumbing, learned from dad in putting in the new bathroom, to dramatics with the high school theater club, or office skills learned from summer jobs. But probably most important of all are the so-called people-skills, both brought to and learned on the job, as Jim discovered in the old CCC.   However, all background skills are valuable and can be used in a service experience.

Team-based vs. Solo-based? This question is not the same as solo-living vs. community living. Members of the faith-based corps live in community but work solo. They each go off to their respective jobs every day. Whereas members of the urban corps work in teams but they often live solo unless they deliberately agree to find an apartment together as Bill and his four housemates did in City Year. Community life is not built into the experience. Peace Corps and VISTA are usually solo living and solo jobs although volunteers may be assigned to a site together and hence live and work together. The advantage, of course, for community living as well as for team-based work, is that both can build an *esprit de corps*. This is a significant feature in a corps experience and is deliberately built into a number of service programs developed by other nations.[12]

Battle with the Beast

Are you worthy yet to pass into adulthood?

This touchstone is the heart of the rite of passage because it is the ultimate test of the mettle of the young person. All young people will test themselves at one point or another, sometimes with deliberate consciousness of what they are doing, but often with little or no awareness. If you do choose a service experience, be aware that you will be testing yourself. In your choice of a service experience, consider the following:

• Think about the most difficult situation you have faced up to this point. How did you deal with it?

- Any one of the following may become a major challenge:

  Isolation
  Loneliness
  Poverty
  Language
  Prejudice
  Food
  Health
  Sexual issues

- Think about your support system:

  What you can bring: your religious faith or philosophy of life, your relationship to your family and friends, your skills in analysis and reflection

  What you can expect a good program to offer: staff mentoring and support, new skills (practical life skills, job skills, and analytical skills)

Past Difficult Situations? When considering a challenge ahead, it's helpful to recognize how you dealt with difficult situations in the past. Look for a pattern. If you have not encountered difficult situations, your life has been too easy and too comfortable. The challenges you will inevitably encounter in a service experience may overwhelm you. Crucial to growing up is recognizing that all lives have difficulties.

As a teenager I lived a sheltered and fairly comfortable life; academics, physical abilities, and social skills came easily. As a result, when I did encounter difficulties, I thought it was because I was too weak, too stupid, or too incompetent to deal with these obstacles rather than because that was simply the nature of life challenging me to do battle with the beast. And I was too embarrassed to tell anyone. If I could have talked about it, I might have found a guardian spirit to warn me that life pulls all of us forward to maturity by "putting brambles in the path," so to speak. It took me years of some painful ordeals to realize that. Here is where the guardian spirit, whatever form it may take, can be so helpful by offering insight, support, and guidance.

Major Challenges? Isolation, loneliness, poverty, language, prejudice, food, health, sexual issues. It is likely that you will encounter most if not every one of these challenges. A lot depends on where you do your service and where in the cycle of your term you are. For instance, isolation and loneliness, and perhaps language and food will be very painful challenges during the first three months. During the middle of the term, poverty, prejudice, and health may emerge as more important. You have been there long enough for the high drama of your work to have subsided and for the mundane aspects to take over. You have perhaps become a little careless about health protection; your presence is no longer a novelty and prejudice emerges; and poverty is no longer romantic but annoying.

Sexual issues can emerge at any point and can involve anything from sexual harassment from members of the opposite sex with different cultural mores, as Don's female peers encountered in Ecuador; to worry about a boyfriend or girlfriend back home, as Sam agonized over when he was serving his Mormon mission; to romances developing within a community house that can upset the whole dynamic of the group. Barbara recalled the warning from her JVC orientation: "Just because you're in the Jesuit Volunteer Corps doesn't mean you can't get pregnant."

These are all real problems, real challenges, and demand some thought.

Support System? The best way to think about these kinds of challenges is to consider what kind of support system you can bring to bear. All of us need effective help when dealing with challenges. Rather than waiting for the crisis, consider ahead of time what can you bring to the experience.

Your religious faith or philosophy of life is central to how you will deal with any challenge because it provides the frame or lens through which you will view the crisis. Have you carefully thought about what you really believe and what your basic values are, where you will draw the line and where you are open to flexibility?

Also important are your relationships to your family and friends. Can you call your mom and dad, for instance, when your world feels like it's collapsing and cry on their shoulder without having them go into a panic and insist you come home immediately? Do you have friends you can trust with your secret anxieties? Have you developed your skills in analysis and reflection so you can pull back from a situation and think it through without hysteria?

What can you expect a good program to offer? Certainly staff mentoring and support. Your project should be offering you new skills: practical life skills, job skills, and analytical skills. Find out if your program of interest provides an educational program, training in leadership skills, and teaches reflection as an important aspect of the experience. Above all, if you expect this experience to be a real rite of passage, don't expect it to be comfortable, because if it's real, it won't be.

Victory

What could my victory possibly be?

Sometimes the only way to get through a difficult time is to think of the rewards of meeting the challenge. A number of the people interviewed for this book take great pride in simply surviving "the most difficult time of my life." But there are other rewards as well, such as self-confidence and self-respect. It is impossible to say ahead of time what your particular "beast" will be and therefore impossible to predict your particular "victory." Be assured, it will have something to do with new knowledge, whether that is competence in job-related skills, expanded horizons regarding the rich diversity of human nature, or a growth in a kind of life-wisdom that will give a depth to your character for the rest of your life.

- Think about the rewards of meeting a challenge:
  Increased self-esteem
  New skills
  Expanded horizons
  Greater knowledge
  Probably greater physical strength
  Heightened awareness
  Diminished prejudice
  Assurance of having earned adulthood
  Perhaps a discovery of your vocation in life

- New opportunities for education and jobs:
  because of additional skills and experience;
  because of greater self-knowledge and self-
      discipline.

Return

How do you come out of an experience like this?

The return is every bit as important as the "guardian spirit," the "task," and the "battle with the beast." Coming out of the experience is a critical time psychologically and should bring with it some sense of closure and celebration.

What do the programs you are considering have to offer in terms of the following:

- Closure

- Celebration

- Opportunities for sharing

- Post-service benefits

Closure. Find out if your program of interest has some form of closure event. City Year calls it "graduation" and it occurs at the same time of year as an academic graduation. The Jesuit Volunteer Corps calls it "dis-orientation"—as opposed to orientation. The Lutheran Volunteer Corps has a final retreat, one of the four that have taken place during the year.

Peace Corps has a closure session in-country for terminating volunteers. The opportunity for debriefing gives the Corps insights for strengthening the program. VISTA has no closure event but sends a certificate through the mail. I received mine months after my term had come to an end. Its arrival in the mail made me aware that I had never quite brought my experience to closure. However, what is important in VISTA—and part of the VISTA philosophy—is for volunteers to make themselves dispensable, preferably with members of the community taking over their jobs. In my case, a new VISTA volunteer came in. I spent the last month of my term training her as well as working with community volunteers.

In Carol's case with VISTA in Montana, she worked with a young Northern Cheyenne woman who came to work at the government agency. Carol helped her become familiar with the process of funding and how to alert the tribes of its availability.

Sharing. The Peace Corps has a strong alumni association and a network with the school systems that calls on returned volunteers to give talks and slide programs on their international experiences. Often a school will have a connection with a Peace Corps member still in the field and set up a pen-pal relationship between the children of the two countries. Churches often call on returned volunteers from the faith-based programs to speak at their churches and schools and to help with recruitment.

Benefits. The hope is that one enters a corps with a desire to give something to the larger world. Yet the interviews indicated to me that the motivation to join the corps may be a real mixed bag to begin with: a desire to escape the draft or to postpone paying off college debts, to enhance one's resume or simply boredom with life the way it is. Regardless of ulterior motives, dedication can grow along with the gift of service. What seems to happen, however, is that satisfaction from the experience is directly correlated to the level of dedication.

Still, it makes sense to look into the kinds of post-service benefits that may come with your term of service: scholarships, fellowships, job preference. After considering all of these factors, the next step is to call or write specific corps and request the latest information.

Finally, keep in mind: What is good for you is good for our community, good for our country, and good for our world. All that is needed is a willing spirit and the right opportunity.

* * *

Chapter Eight

The Journey Beckons:
What Opportunities Are Available?

The parallel piece to the young person's responsibility to earn the right to adulthood is the community's responsibility to provide opportunities for that to happen. The youth crisis tells us this is a necessity not a luxury. The labor market and educational system, for complex reasons, are not as able as they once were to help young people grow up. Therefore, a new institution can and must become a realistic bridge from adolescence to adulthood.[1] Youth service might well serve that purpose. Although not the only means, it may be the best.

One task on the road to adulthood is learning the skills of identifying, using wisely, and conserving resources. So too the United States must grow out of its own cultural adolescence and stop its profligate use and abuse of resources. The most shameless abuse of resources is that of its young people. Until we salvage our youth from this throw-away mentality and treasure them as the valuable resources they are, our nation will not mature and our young people will not grow up. Both must develop together.

Here are some scenarios for how that can happen, again framed by the metaphor of the heroic journey and its touchstones.

The Call

How can we ensure that young people will find out about service corps options?

Social maturity begins when young people feel compelled to expand their world, not by taking to the street with a gang nor by prematurely conceiving a child, but by looking at diverse options for service opportunities. But this must be a realistic possibility.

One scenario suggests that all young women as well as young men might register when they reach age 17, just as 18-year-old men do now. At that time they could obtain packets of information on civilian and military options open to them.[2] Posters in local stores, public service announcements on radio and television, directories at the neighborhood and school libraries, guidance counselors, teachers, and clergy could provide additional information. Moreover, because they already have had service-learning opportunities in school, they will have developed some of the skills they can use in moving into a full-time term of service.

However, there must be a critical mass of young people engaged in youth corps, so the public at large will both know of their existence and see their impact.[3] The possibilities offered by the corps should be apparent to all young people, not that they be required to participate but that they realize they have the opportunity.

"Opportunity," was originally a nautical term. It referred to a wind coming at the right time to blow a ship into port. So, every young person needs an experience to come along at the right time in life to help "blow" him or her into adulthood. Neither a mere breeze nor a typhoon is appropriate. A harbor cannot long survive shipwrecks. The appropriate opportunities must be there and information about them easily available.

In an ideal situation:

- There should be sufficient programs and adequate variety to appeal to a wide range of young people from various cultural and religious backgrounds.

- There should be a national network to inform, promote quality, and offer various kinds of support to programs and youth in all parts of the country.[4]

- A variety of programs should welcome and encourage young people from all backgrounds to participate.

- Both full-time and part-time programs should be an option.

- Both domestic and international experiences should be open.

The Departure

What kind of support is the community able and willing to give for the sake of its young people responding to the call?

Leaving home is not easy, even under the best—or worst—of circumstances. A young person needs the financial wherewithal, and the skill to use it wisely, as well as an emotional anchor to ensure a healthy separation.

Regarding financial support, the high cost of education and technical training is quickly moving out of reach even for middle-class parents. Paying for a youth corps experience in addition to higher education or technical training is often an unreasonable stretch. This is especially true when there are other children in the family to educate and the needs of the parents' retirement hovering on the horizon. Moreover, this is the time when young people should begin to terminate financial dependence on parents.

As Doris, who has spent 50 years of her life as a volunteer Red Cross nurse, points out, "Volunteering is a luxury, reserved for those of us who are supported by someone else." She is grateful to her husband for making it possible for her to volunteer her service all these years but realizes that it is not possible for many people who have both the skills and the desire to do the same.

Think of the irony of a term like volunteer service in the context of a temporary, full-time commitment, such as the youth corps offer. "Voluntary" comes ultimately from the Latin, *volo,* meaning "I will." Yet without some kind of financial support, the reality is "I can't."

Furthermore, we need to shed the idea that a stipend for a term of service is simply another government hand-out. Is it not reasonable to pay for legitimate work?[5] Not for raking leaves, as the cartoonists would have us believe, but for important work that will go undone if not taken on by young people who are willing to dedicate themselves to the tasks. The Ford Foundation in 1986 identified useful assignments that would be appropriate for thousands of young servers.[6] We must learn to perceive our young people in terms of resource development and support them so they can give what they have to offer. It's a two-way street: both sides contributing to the benefit of the whole.

To give substance to the emotional anchor, so necessary for a successful trip to adulthood, the corps should—and many do—incorporate into their program community-building skills. On the one hand, this will enable the young Achilles of the nation to find the sense of family they so desperately hunger for in new, but emotionally-necessary, experiences of being needed. On the other hand, the young preppies of the nation will have healthier options than boozing in the fraternity and sorority houses in order to bond with their brothers and sisters. They too need to be needed and challenged in healthier ways.

The families of adolescents and the community at large must work together to pinpoint the best timing for a service experience. This can vary widely from person to person and community to community. My own experience tells me that taking time for a corps experience right after high school or early in my college career would have been of immense help to me. For one thing, I might have avoided switching majors three times because I would have gained a more realistic sense of the world out there and of what I might have to offer.

Just as important, young people tempted to drop out of high school can find a legitimate alternative, a way to interrupt a negative series of events by discovering how to contribute something positive and, in the process, learning important lessons and completing their GED.

Young people who do have a corps experience, or something similar at that time of life, seem to come into technical school or college with greater focus and direction. Colleges and tech schools would do well to find out what kind of impact the corps have on returning students' academic work. Certainly the GI Bill proved the impact of maturity on the academic achievement of older students.

There may be some lessons from religious communities as well that have held service as an expectation for their young people.

The Mormon Experience. The consensus regarding the best age for mission work within the Mormon community has evolved over time. Sam, who went to Samoa in 1960 as a Mormon missionary, reminds us that,

> When the church was young during the 19th century, the missionaries were primarily the older married men. Eventually, during the 20th century, the church decided to call young men to go. Until 1960 the minimum age was 20. Then the church lowered the age to 19. The general expectation is that every worthy male member of the church at the age of 19 will serve a mission.

The Latter-day Saints place great value on the mission experience, both for the sake of the development of their youth and for the sake of the community's religious well-being. When the parents cannot afford it, other adults in the community help pay the price. This is an example of a coherent community committed to a valuable "right of passage." The community as a whole ensures that it takes place . . . and—by the way—benefits from its investment.

The Mennonite Experience. The Mennonites believe that service is integral to their Christian faith. Therefore the very expression of their faith demands that they feed the hungry, educate the poor, help developing communities, and bring down barriers that would prevent peace.

In 1920 the Mennonite Central Committee (MCC) came into being to respond to war-related human needs. It grew rapidly during World War II to deal with the increased need for service, especially in relief and refugee programs.

As a peace church the Mennonites sought alternative service options for conscientious objectors. They continue to this day to work in developing countries to meet the needs, both physical and spiritual, of the people.

The MCC offers a wide range of service opportunities, from three-month to three-year assignments. For the two- and three-year assignments the MCC provides the total cost, including medical expense and round-trip transportation, plus a modest monthly stipend. For shorter assignments the participants are responsible for sharing the cost of the experience.

A philosophy of service has infused the curriculum of Goshen College, a Mennonite liberal arts college in Goshen, Indiana. During the mid-'60s the college introduced a new requirement for graduation: the Study-Service Term (SST). Beginning in 1968 all students had the opportunity to spend a trimester in a culture quite different from that of the U.S. engaged in study and field (i.e., service) experience. Erika did her SST in the late '80s in Costa Rica. The tuition for the SST is the same as it would be if living on campus.

The Jesuit Experience. The Jesuit Volunteer Corps started in 1956 (five years before the Peace Corps) when a Jesuit missionary in Alaska appealed for help in his school for Eskimos. The response surprised him. More were willing to come than he could use, but, as a wise steward of resources, he found additional sites for the overflow.

Since then close to 7,000 volunteers have participated in the domestic and international corps. The Jesuit Volunteer Corps depends to a great extent on their communities for support. The domestic corps derives about 50 percent of its support from the agencies drawing on the volunteers. The other 50 percent comes from appeals to the

JVC alumni and alumni families, the families of present volunteers, Catholic parishes, grants for specific programs, and general appeals. The Jesuit Volunteers International, on the other hand, depends more heavily on direct appeals from Catholic parishes and from private contributions.[7]

The Lutheran Experience. The Luther Place Church in Washington, D.C. founded the Lutheran Volunteer Corps (LVC) in 1979. The intent was to offer opportunities to people who were willing to commit themselves to a year of full-time urban service in the nation's capital. In the past decade and a half the LVC has expanded to seven urban centers.

Founded on the Jesuit and Mennonite model, the Lutheran Volunteer Corps members live in community, accept a simple life style, and work for social justice and spiritual growth. As with the JVC, a variety of sources support the LVC: about 33 percent from placement agencies, about 20 percent from grants, and the rest from the national Evangelical Lutheran Church in America and the synods that contain LVC houses. From 1979 to 1994 the LVC has placed slightly over 700 volunteers.[8]

Other Programs. The corps have continued to grow. Other organizations, too, are sending young (and older) people into homes for the elderly, children's day care centers, shelters and soup kitchens for the homeless, prisons, reservations: places where needs would go unmet if they were not served by people willing to give a year or two of their lives to such service. Some additional programs include the following: The Christian Brothers Volunteer program, the Edmundite Teacher Corps, the Franciscan Service Program, the Holy Cross Volunteers, the Mercy Corps, the Vincentian Service Corps, and the United Methodist Volunteers. Yet all of these faith-based programs are merely a "drop in the bucket" compared with the size of the national programs.

National Programs. The Civilian Conservation Corps and the Peace Corps are examples of a U.S. national investment in youth service. At its peak in the mid-1930s the CCC enrolled 500,000 young men a year. In 1942 when the program ended, it had served nearly 3 million participants and reaped the benefit of millions of dollars worth of constructive work. In contrast, the Peace Corps had enrolled a total of only 130,000 as of 1990. VISTA, during its 30 years, has never exceeded 5,500 at one time. Yet, is there anyone today who would doubt the value of these experiences, both to the young people involved as well as to the country at large? . . . and to the world for that matter? These too are examples of programs where the returns are greater than the investment.[9]

The variety and diversity of programs are healthy and good. Almost any interest and inclination should find just the right opportunity. The problem is there are not enough of them. If one were to àdd up all the slots available in all of the corps right now, they would represent opportunities for only a fraction of all the young people between the ages of 18 and 24 in the nation today.

We would be foolish to expect the government to provide all of the opportunities for service to young people; we have never done that. We would be equally foolish, on the contrary, to expect the churches to carry the full burden for all of the young people in the nation, especially when many of the nation's young people who could most benefit are not members of a religious community. The concept of national service must be far more than a federal program. It must be a national commitment to service opportunities of all kinds, open to all young Americans who choose to participate.

It's obvious that the people who have something at stake in the maturation of our young must figure out a way to support that process. The reality is we *all* have a stake. We all need to figure out a way to support our young people in their passage to adulthood.

A Scenario. In an ideal situation, young people will receive information on corps options. They will discuss possibilities with their parents, perhaps a teacher or two or a guidance counselor, maybe a chaplain or member of the clergy. After making up their minds, they will leave home to begin the corps experience. They should be able to expect the following:

- Since separation from home is an important part of a rite of passage, youth corps programs should put emphasis on providing adequate, safe, and healthy residential programs.

- Both options—living alone or in a community—have value, but the choice demands careful consideration and can spell the difference between success and failure of the experience for a young person. Adequate orientation to the challenges of each is essential.

- If this is not a tuition-based college program, a living stipend is necessary and appropriate. Otherwise, only the wealthy can afford it. The perception that young people are being "paid for volunteer work" is faulty. We would not expect our youth to go into the military service without a living stipend. Similarly we should not expect that in a youth service corps.

Encounter with the Guardian Spirit

Is the community willing to play its role in inspiring, orienting, and mentoring young people as they prepare themselves to move into adulthood?

Young people who have decided to enter a corps will undergo an orientation that will prepare them to deal with the challenges of the experience. They will come together in a place apart from their homes and work sites to get to know each other and their corps leaders and supervisors. A well-designed orientation will help them recognize that their presence and skills are important to the task they will undertake. Peer bonding is important. Periodic retreats, meetings, newsletters, or whatever is appropriate for a given corps should support these new relationships. Contrary to being superfluous, the bond can be integral to the learning process and emotional satisfaction during the term of service.

The orientation should introduce certain skills: proper attention to health (including nutrition and hygiene); interpersonal skills (including basic etiquette and conflict resolution); methods of dealing with difficult situations; and reflection techniques. A certain amount of social inoculation should take place during orientation. Young people need to prepare for the possibility of insensitive work supervisors, intercultural misunderstanding, including possible sexual harassment, ill-designed job descriptions, and health and safety hazards.

Young people need to know how to identify potential mentors when they get to their work sites. At the same time we adults must recognize the importance of looking after young people who enter our realm of life. Connection between the generations can take many forms:

personal mentoring, tutoring, providing jobs, corporate sponsorship of youth corps. The example of City Year draws attention to ways in which the business world can support youth service through corporate sponsorship. The responsibility of the youth corps, of course, is adequately-trained and well-intentioned leaders.

The orientation at the beginning of a term of service sets the tone for the whole year to come. A youth corps member should be able to expect the following:

- Critical to a good program is appropriate background and adequate training of the corps leaders.

- Current programs should integrate the lessons learned from past programs.

- Corps leadership should consider periodic retreats a valuable addition to a corps experience, a supplement to the initial orientation.

- Adults must increase their awareness of the importance of caring for young people in whatever ways are appropriate to their occupation and life situation.

Taking on the Task

What kind of jobs are appropriate for the youth corps? Is the community willing to provide such tasks and train young people to do them?

The various youth corps develop yearly job lists that include brief job descriptions, the expected background and skills, the location, and dates. Some corps, like VISTA and the Mennonites, have rolling admissions. Others like City Year and the Jesuit and Lutheran Volunteer Corps follow fairly close to an academic calendar. This may have a bearing on choice. Keep in mind the following considerations:

- Young people coming into the corps should expect to find a fairly accurate job description, yet one open to individual adaptation.

- The corps leader should ensure skill development adequate for the task.

- The corps should be flexible enough to take advantage of background experiences the young people bring with them.

- The corps should recognize the advantages and disadvantages of team-based and solo-based work and prepare its members to handle whichever they take on. Ideally they will experience some of both.

- The corps must make sure the tasks are *real work* serving real needs. Nothing will sour someone on service faster than make-work.

Battle with the Beast

Is the community willing to challenge young people to help them become truly worthy to pass into adulthood?

The corps should prepare its participants to deal with "the beasts" they are likely to encounter: challenges such as isolation, loneliness, poverty, language, prejudice, food, health, and sexual issues. When young people understand that it's normal to experience difficulties, they will be less apt to think there is something wrong with them and to give up too soon. They will discover that growth comes from being stretched.

Young corps members may not realize that they bring support systems with them to an experience: their religious faith and philosophy of life, their relationships to their family and friends, their skills in analysis and reflection. Corps leaders must understand this and be trained to help their youthful charges learn how to take advantage of such support. After all, "doing battle" can actually strengthen support systems in a young life.

- Based on past experience, corps leaders should identify the "beasts" in the challenges they offer their participants. During orientation they should prepare corps members for the potential "battles" they may face.

- One of the most daunting, yet most important, challenges is that of working together with people of other social, racial, and ethnic backgrounds. For the well-being of the country as a whole, as well as full human development of our young people, the mechanisms for this to happen must be in place.

- Young people must learn how to identify and to make healthy use of the support systems in their lives to help them survive their "battles" successfully.

Victory

What can the community do to help insure the opportunity for "victory" for all young people?

American culture tends to focus so much on the externals of life that we seldom think about our inner world until we are shocked into awareness by a crisis. For this reason some kind of "battle with the beast" seems to be a developmental necessity. It will happen without being deliberately set up. A truly challenging task will by its nature entail some kind of "battle."

The "victory" is a sharpened awareness stimulated by the "battle": an awareness that I am a giver, not a taker; that I choose to be a we, not just a me;[10] that each of us has a gift to bring to, not steal from life. We demonstrate the truth of this awareness by our acts of service deliberately chosen. Furthermore, the community must confirm our realization. This new understanding causes a shift in perspective in both the youth and the community. This is why such transformations have demanded some kind of rite or celebration: to give them the attention they deserve.

A rite, from one perspective, is a form of "Reflection with a capital R"; it is a way to slow down an experience psychologically in order to reflect on it and "digest" it. There are, however, many forms of "small r" reflection, and the corps should be teaching reflection techniques to ensure that its members will derive the benefits of surviving a crisis.

The young corps members who fought forest fires despite immense fear, who helped build up war-torn Europe despite emotional revulsion, who taught biology despite culture shock, who created bonds with refugee children despite faltering language skills, who sorted out resources for the homeless despite bureaucratic confusion, can't help but come out of such experiences with increased self-esteem, new interpersonal and job skills, greater self-discipline, and assurance of having earned adulthood. This is a strong foundation for building a life as a citizen as well as for building a career.

It is, however, only in recent years that the corps are recognizing the importance of reflection to the service experience. Without it, service is a nice thing to do—better done than not done—but with it, the service experience transforms people.

A cartoon from the time of the early Clinton administration shows two frames. In the top frame, said to be earlier in the Bush administration, a young man with a white tee-shirt and black mortarboard pushes a broom. He is described as depressed. In the bottom frame the same youth is wearing a white National Youth Service tee-shirt and his black mortarboard. Now, however, he is described as inspired and not depressed. He is still pushing his broom.[11] What an example of re-framing one's experience, even though intended as satire.

Another example of the power of a frame of reference is a medieval French parable:

> A hermit was walking down the road and came upon a
> man carving a stone. The hermit stopped and asked,
> "What are you doing?" The man replied, "Carving a
> stone." The hermit continued on his way and soon came
> upon another man doing the same thing. The hermit
> asked, "What are you doing?" The man replied,
> "Earning a living." The hermit continued walking and
> came upon a third man carving away. The hermit asked,
> "What are you doing?" The third man replied, "Building
> a cathedral."[12]

Young people in youth service are engaged not just in low-paying jobs but in building their world. Such a frame-shift turns drudgery into exhilaration. I've seen it happen. Doris is an example. She took on jobs as a Red Cross nurse "that you could not have paid me to do." Frame-shifts like these come out of the power and insight of reflection.

The frame-shift transforms because it enables a person to see a situation in a significantly different way. When Steve came to recognize the difference between his wants and his needs during his Peace Corps term in Togo; when Sam realized that he could be deathly ill without the presence of his family; when Julie could empathize with her unsympathetic supervising teacher in Anchorage; when Barbara could help resolve the conflicts with her housemates in Dallas in spite of her own initial prejudice: Each experienced a transformation. This was possible because they had re-framed their perspective.

Many of the early corps did not recognize and emphasize the importance of reflection. Yet from the beginning the Peace Corps made a practice of sending footlockers of books with its volunteers. Those who read them were stimulated to reflect on their adopted culture. Young people who went into the faith-based corps found themselves reflecting during sharing-time with their housemates, whether they were conscious of it or not. The commitment to community and spirituality, peace and justice, by its nature, demands a certain amount of reflection.

Some of the participants in this story admitted they had not thought about certain issues until I confronted them with particular questions. So the reflection was after-the-fact. Fortunately, it was before they had forgotten-the-fact. Others told me they had kept a journal and were often surprised when they went back to read it and discovered incidents and feelings they had forgotten.

Reflection is the flavor-enhancer of an experience. It gives a sharpened definition to an experience and helps us identify where we draw the frames of our lives. Why is this important? Because we experience the picture of reality that we frame. Through reflection we discover where we need to redraw those frames so that we can transform ourselves. To help this process, the following should happen:

- The community must put forth healthy challenges for all of our youth and ensure that adequate training in necessary work and people skills as well as in reflection is built into the corps experience.

- Corps members should come out of their service experience with an increased understanding of the relevance of their work to the community as a whole. Why was their service important and what difference did it make to the lives of the people with whom they worked?

- Corps should help their members prepare for new opportunities in education and jobs as a result of their corps experience.

Return

How does the community celebrate and mark the completion of its young people's term of service?

Closure. Many of the corps now recognize the importance of a closure experience, whether it is a debriefing session, a final retreat, a graduation, or a party.

For example, many corps members are even advised how to make the most of their closure experience so that it will be as positive as possible. The City Year graduation each June may be the most public of the closure experiences. It is also a celebration.

Celebration. Perhaps the most thoughtful of the ceremonies was one practiced in Pennsylvania in the late 1980s. The governor's office recognized the new status as adult citizens of young people who had completed their term in a service corps. Modeled on the new citizen's ceremony, the youth corps graduates took the oath of citizenship and received citizenship cards signed by the governor. This secular ritual was a public celebration of what the young people had accomplished. In addition, it was a maturity marker, a public recognition of their new adult relationship with their state and their country. A later administration dropped the practice, but other forms of celebration continue.

Opportunities for Sharing. The religious communities have a built-in sharing opportunity as a way of acknowledging and thanking the communities that have helped support the young person in the field. The returning corps member is invited so speak to church groups and sometimes even in the church itself. Again, the public recognition for what has been accomplished is a significant marker. Alumni groups are a good support system for those who find their former friends less than interested in what has happened to them.

Post-service Benefits. Many of the corps, like City Year and the City Volunteer Corps of New York, award an educational stipend at the completion of their term: a $5,000 college scholarship or a $2,500 cash payment.

Others, like Peace Corps and VISTA, offer a transition stipend. My VISTA stipend, awarded at the end of my term in 1992, amounted to $833 after taxes.

One of the appeals of the AmeriCorps program is the financial reward for college or vocational school tuition or loans. Young people can get their education first and then do their service. That sequence of activity, however, may not be the best idea. Don Eberly, founder of the National Service Secretariat—as well as others in the service movement—believes that the reward should come *after* the service, as was true of the original GI Bill.

Graduate fellowships are often available for those who have been in the service corps. Both the skills they have gained while serving as well as the dedication to a higher cause make them attractive candidates. Many colleges and universities openly admit now that they look with favor on those applicants with service experience. VISTA and Peace Corps alumni have a one-year favored status in applying for federal jobs. Peace Corps newsletters carry a job column to enable returned volunteers to re-enter the job market as easily as possible. Research also finds that Peace Corps alumni have a significantly lower unemployment rate.[13]

In spite of a one-year preference for federal jobs, former VISTAs have told me that apart from government work, they get little recognition in the job pool because VISTA has carried such a low profile over a good part of its existence. Even people who know about it, have said to me, "I thought that program ended years ago." So those coming out of a term of service, unless it was in the Peace Corps, should not count on their experience providing entry to a job in the general public. Nevertheless, service alumni are frequently hired as regular staff members by the agencies they served, or they often step into jobs with the corps itself because of their valuable experience and their directly relevant skills.

The challenge for each of the service corps is to offer some kind of preparation for returning to the regular world after a term of service. City Year conducts sessions on resume writing, interviewing, and other life skills essential for making one's way in the world. The Saint Vincent Pallotti Center in Washington, D.C. has produced *The "What's Next?" Notebook* which offers suggestions, strategies, and general tips for returning to the "real" world to the faith-based corps alumni[14] The government programs would do well to learn from the private corps for supportive ways to bring their corps members "home."

A National Stake in Service

Why the big emphasis on service corps at this time in our national history?

It's only common sense to recognize that when life-conditions change, the body politic must adjust to fit the circumstances. The youth crisis tells us that from the perspective of young people trying to grow up today, the labor market and education system, once considered the American bridge to adulthood, are no longer adequate. Other institutions must be identified or created to serve that role. A youth service corps experience can be one of the most effective.

From the perspective of the adult world, serious needs are going unmet, and the resources to meet them are growing less available. Consider the following: More wives and mothers—long the back-bone of volunteerism—are now working part- or full-time. Young professionals are discovering longer work-weeks the rule rather than the exception. Greater mobility reduces the amount of time spent in the home community, both because of longer commutes to work and because of job-related travel demands. For goodness sake, even the bowling leagues are dying out.

How then is the community going to take up the slack, especially at a time when the federal government is cutting subsidies for social services? How are young people going to grow up without the support of the community at large, helping them channel their energy and curiosity, protecting them from exploitation, and giving them the message that they are needed?

No society can long exist without ways to reinforce the web of constructive relationships. This is what service opportunities and social and civic organizations represent. When these relationships are not sustained, the society breaks apart. When they are in place, a society is knit together. What better way to build and sustain human relationships than to provide ways for young people to bring their energy, their ideas, and their enthusiasm to work on necessary tasks with people they would otherwise never meet?

Although many paths exist on the journey to adulthood, there are reasons why some paths may be better than others. We as a nation had better take another look at the critical role of youth service at this point in our history.

* * *

Chapter Nine

Getting There:
Why Some Paths May Be Better
Than Others

P eople often ask, "How does a service experience differ from an internship or apprenticeship, a work-study or study abroad program?" There is no simple answer because there can be considerable overlap among these various types of experiences. Each in its own way can be a significant push into maturity because they all help develop skills and qualities of character necessary for adulthood. However, the purpose of each is somewhat different, and that can affect the attitude of and the impact on the young person going through the program.

Work-Study

The work-study program usually refers to one of two possibilities: a job that a college student on financial aid works a certain number of hours each week for minimum wages, or an off-campus full-time, temporary job which the student alternates with full-time academic work. The first is often menial (washing dishes, setting up chairs for programs, filing and photocopying in department offices); the second may be professional (working in a chemical lab or architectural firm, for instance).

The first is usually labor to put up with in order to pay for college; the second can be a labor of love to prepare for a life's profession. They both help pay for college. The first reinforces the role of student; the second invites the student into the role of professional. Both tend to focus on the self in terms of "What am I getting out of this?" Each may or may not involve reflection, but this is seldom built into the program. The same can be said of the opportunity to experience other cultures. It may happen, but if so, it is more by coincidence than by design.

The original intent of the College Work-Study Program (CWSP)[1] was to fight poverty in two ways: through financial aid to needy students and through the assignment of those students to poverty areas to do the "work" part of the "work-study." But eventually financial aid offices on campus captured the students and assigned them to such tasks as washing dishes and filing departmental documents on campus. Serving the poor off-campus has never engaged more than 15 percent of work-study students, which is a pretty feeble response to its original intent.[2]

Ellen, who graduated from a southern university in 1988, spent her first year in a college work-study program working in a civil rights research center, at the time loosely affiliated with her university, but located off-campus. "The majority of the jobs were on-campus." She recalls:

> Most of the jobs, including mine, were doing nothing but Xeroxing, collating, and stapling. It was not a

positive experience by any means. It was simply a way to earn $3.35 an hour, which was the minimum wage at that time.

She spent the first semester of her second year in one of the university departments photocopying and collating doctoral dissertations on "stone-age machinery." During the second semester she transcribed interview tapes for a sociology professor. "I guess work-study was good for picking up secretarial skills," she muses, "but other than that, it was a mindless, tedious, soul-destroying task."

Robert had a more positive experience at a western liberal arts college where he spent three years working in the audio-visual department doing set-ups for lectures, films, and concerts. He came to the work-study job with a basic knowledge of video and sound equipment and left the experience with considerably increased knowledge. Not only did he gain free admission to all the programs he serviced, but his first post-college professional-level job as a financial analyst for broadcast companies came not because of his major in political science but as a result of his familiarity with audio-visual equipment.

The College Work-Study Program (CWSP) is a mixed bag. For some it can turn out to be an apprenticeship for a career; for others it can be "slave labor." While an essential subsidy for students who could not otherwise attend their chosen college, work-study programs should balance tedious tasks with those that engage the young student with the community so that such jobs can enlighten rather than deaden the emerging adult.

Joan had the second type of work-study experience: a combination of classroom study and professional work related to her discipline. During her five years at a large Midwestern university, where she majored in chemistry during the 1970s, she spent alternate terms working in a chemical laboratory in a nearby city. The experience not only helped pay her tuition but gave her a valuable addition to her resume upon graduation. In Joan's experience the connection between her study and work was not as tight as that in a true internship.

Internship

The internship is usually integrated into a high school or college academic program or post-graduate program. The image of young doctors as interns often comes to mind. Allen Wutzdorff, director of the National Society for Experiential Education describes an internship as "any experience in a work setting that is driven by intentional learning goals and accompanied by sustained reflection."[3] It provides the student with the opportunity to move out of the classroom. For a stipulated amount of time the student works under the guidance of a professional in a field of interest. The site supervisor cooperates with the academic advisor regarding the expectations of the student. Depending on the length of time in the internship, the student may well remain in the role of student. However, given the maturity of the intern and the length of the internship, the student may move into the role of a professional.

Mentorship is built into the system when it is part of an academic program and may open up a long-term enriching relationship. Reflection is an essential aspect, especially if the intern earns academic credit; but the credit is for the learning achieved not simply for the experience, valuable as that may be. As with a work-study program, cross-cultural contact may or may not be part of the experience.

Internship outside the academic arena, however, is becoming quite common. College graduates frequently expect to spend 6 to 12 months in an internship, often for little or no pay—what some of the them call "free labor." It is one way to "get a foot in the door" in a tight job market.[4]

Apprenticeship

The apprenticeship has a long and rich history. The idea goes at least as far back as the ancient Sumerians, Greeks, and Romans, but most of us probably came in contact with the concept when studying the guilds of medieval Europe.[5] The young person would enter a relationship with a master artisan around the age of puberty. He would work in the craft for a certain number of years until he could demonstrate adequate proficiency, at which time he would become a journeyman. If and when he became the owner of his own business, he might be eligible to be a master himself. The guilds, especially in Germany, kept tight control of standards and practices within the craft. To this day, Germany has a well-regarded apprenticeship system.

The use of the term is sometimes synonymous with internship. Usually internship is embedded in an academic program (as is the case with the young doctor), and apprenticeship takes place after the young person has left school (as is the case with young people learning their craft from the trade unions). The role-shift from student to professional can take place to the extent that the young person's growing skills and his or her work supervisor allows.

The terminology, however, becomes complicated because the School-to-Work programs are describing the work component as an apprenticeship rather than an internship. Moreover, "internships" for college graduates occur after the graduates have left the classroom.

So, rather than the formal structure, it is the outcome of the program that marks the distinction between internships and apprenticeships. Both apprenticeships and internships provide training, but internships are attached to professions and apprenticeships to trades. The one-to-one relationship between the young person and the older mentor may or may not be stressed in both the internship and apprenticeship models.

The development of work skills and appropriate behavior habits are specifically defined for the apprentice. Reflection may or may not happen, depending on the propensity of both the apprentice and the work supervisor. Apprentices may or may not learn to see and understand the context of their work: They may or may not be able to see how it is part of a wider social system and understand its role in the bigger picture of their culture at large. Work supervisors—hopefully mentors—would be wise to encourage this kind of reflection. But the ultimate goal of the apprentice is to gain the necessary work skills and knowledge to begin the ascent on the career ladder.

Stephen Hamilton, an expert on the German model of apprenticeship, has suggested an American counterpart.[6] His idea is to integrate community service and youth corps experience into a comprehensive apprenticeship system. As he suggests, such a program would not only instill work virtues and skills more effectively, it could radically reform education. He points out that teaching and learning should not be confined to the school building but should be deliberately dispersed throughout a community.[7]

Ideas like this have had such an impact on public policy that by early 1994 a School-to-Work Opportunities Act was signed into law. It provides funding to help support job-related programs: career academies for public high school students which specialize in careers such as automotive repair, environmental technology, health, hotel and restaurant management, law, and physical education; "tech prep" experiments, which emphasize technology-related courses; and youth apprenticeship initiatives in which students work as paid apprentices in local businesses.[8]

The Job Corps

Part of the 1960s War on Poverty, the Job Corps has been one of the most successful of the programs for non-college-bound young people. It has been a federally funded residential (for the most part) training program for unemployed youths. Open to young men and women, between the ages of 16 and 21, it offers training in more than 160 fields. The programs last from six months to two years, depending on the demands of the field. Although some non-residential options exist, most of the participants live in a dormitory setting, not unlike a college campus. The program is free of charge. The participants receive a monthly allowance—$35 a month to begin—which increases with growing seniority. In addition there is a clothing and readjustment allowance. Opportunities are available to prepare for GED and even to begin working toward a college-level Associate of Arts degree.

The strengths of the Job Corps are that it has for 30 years provided essential job skills to low-income young people and has opened up the opportunity to develop the discipline and work habits essential to a successful career. The disadvantage is the limited diversity of participants, the kind of diversity encouraged in a service corps environment.

Public Allies

A creative combination of apprenticeship with community service is expressed in the Public Allies program. In 1991 two young women, Katrina Browne and Vanessa Kirsch, became aware of the cynical attitudes of young people toward the political system and were inspired to found Public Allies. Young people, 18 to 30-years-old, apprentice to non-profit agencies for 10 months and, at the same time, gain experience in team-building, leadership skills, and conflict resolution. Tom, who served as a VISTA volunteer with the Sojourners community, then spent a year as a Public Ally in Washington, D.C. where the program started. Public Allies now live and work in Chicago, Milwaukee, Raleigh-Durham, San Jose, and Wilmington, Del.[9]

Apparent in any discussion of internships and apprenticeships in the United States is what slippery fish they are. Just when you think you have grabbed hold and defined them, they slip away and turn into something else. We simply need to understand that the terms are fairly fluid and therefore depend on the context to convey the precise meaning.

Study-Abroad Programs

The study-abroad program is intercultural by design. In many ways it is an heroic journey. The young exchange student faces the separation and sacrifice of the familiar, taking on the challenge of new customs and often of a new language as well. A significant difference from the overseas service experience is that study abroad usually lacks a role-shift. Study-abroad students come as students and remain as students for the duration of the experience. Yet, even as students he and she face tasks of survival, which they would not encounter on their home campuses. There is a major "occupational hazard" for exchange students, however: to come to the overseas site with a group of peers who remain in their own cultural bubble until they depart.

Both the Association of Episcopal Colleges and The Partnership for Service-Learning (PS-L) offer a creative integration of the study abroad program with community service. A college student has the option of taking a deferment from full-time study and doing full-time service in another culture or doing part-time study and part-time service. Goshen College (Mennonite) has since 1968 required a term of international service-learning for graduation.

In a sense these programs offer the best of both worlds except that the young person is still tied to the academic system.[10] Yet that can also be an advantage: The learning from the service experience in the PS-L, for instance, is structured by the Social Institutions course, an integral part of the program. The course ensures that the service will promote a growing understanding of the social, economic, and political structures of the society within which one is working.

Part-time Volunteer Work

Well, then, one might ask, what about the value of doing part-time service while engaged in school or regular employment? This can be a journey in itself. But there are also inherent weaknesses, given the nature of part-time service. The quality of a service experience depends to a great extent on the preparation, support, and opportunities for reflection on the part of the volunteers.

Ellen spent a year after graduation from college working for a bank in a large urban center. At the same time she volunteered to tutor three to four junior high school youngsters two evenings a week in reading and math. The volunteer center provided a brief orientation and a set curriculum. She recalls that,

> By the time it was over, I felt that I really didn't have anything to offer these kids. There was a huge culture gap; we weren't even speaking the same language. I hope they picked up something from the curriculum, but I'm sorry to say I don't think they got anything positive from me.

She stuck it out until one of the kids who was older and bigger than the others provoked a fight and then threatened to come back and "shoot up the place." The following week there was a counseling session at another site for the rest of the students and tutors. At that point the program stopped for the year—just a few weeks before the end of the school term.

Too often idealistic young people are turned loose to "do their thing" with little or no training and little or no mentoring or support. They can easily be overwhelmed and disillusioned and become convinced that the problems are just too big to solve or that they just don't have the skills to tackle them. Every time this happens, valuable resources and good will are lost.

On the other hand, many high schools, colleges, and universities are building service experience into the curriculum and providing good preparation, strong support, and the discipline of reflection, all of which open up the potential for intensive learning and sharing to take place even under less than ideal conditions.[11] In the process of raising awareness of social needs and making commitments to serve those needs, citizenship and civic responsibility become conscious choices.

Full-time Service

Each of these various paths can lead to maturity, but there are certain values which a full-time service experience can bring to a young life. As a member of a service corps, personal identity is enlarged by social identity. One is no longer simply John or Jane Doe, working on this little project in Boston, or Chicago, or Washington, D.C. One becomes Jane Doe, City Year Volunteer . . . or Public Ally . . . or literacy tutor with VISTA . . . or a leader for a state conservation corps . . . connected to all the other John and Jane Does identified by the same organization. John Doe has not only expanded his own mental horizons, but his identity has been enhanced forever, as were those of the old CCC alumni.

Furthermore, the identity of Jane and John Doe is reinforced by the symbolic nature of the logo, or by the uniform, or even by the very name of the group which often takes on a mystique in the public consciousness. Such symbolism carries a subtle but profound power and can surface in unexpected situations.

The Heroic Myth. Around 1991 Elizabeth, a young playwright, was invited to a college in Poland as a visiting lecturer in drama for a term. When she arrived she was taken to her temporary living quarters, led up a dark, narrow stairway encased with gray concrete walls, to a desolate one-room apartment where she would spend the next three months. As she pulled the string to the bare bulb, depression washed over her like the glare of the light. Attempting to rouse herself out of self-pity, she thought of the invitation which had recently come to the Peace Corps for volunteers to aid Poland's transition to democracy. The more she thought about fellow Americans responding to such a call, the more her spirit rose out of depression.

Because she was able to connect, even if only mentally, with something larger than herself—because she was able to become a participant in an American heroic myth—she garnered the energy to shake off the paralysis of self pity and enter the story of the hero. Her attitude was transformed by that subtle shift in perspective, a new frame of reference. Her three months, although not easy, were immensely rewarding, in no small measure because enlivened and validated by connection to something beyond herself.

Who can deny that the Peace Corps has taken on a mystique? How many American citizens reach mid-life and promise themselves that when and if the situation is right they will join the Peace Corps, or one of the other corps, and contribute their part to the human endeavor. Former President Jimmy Carter's mother, Lillian, became an American heroine when she joined the Peace Corps in her 60s. And now Mr. Carter and his wife, Rosalynn, are themselves identified with Habitat for Humanity.

What is unspoken, and perhaps even unconscious, is the desire for a piece of the heroic journey, which some of us may have bypassed at an earlier point in our lives. Most of us crave adventure. Too often, however, such desire takes the path of the forbidden, the thrill of excessive risk, dilettante tourism, even the urge to buy, buy, buy–evidence that our worlds are too small. What's more, we tend to limit our young people as well to boundaries that are too narrow.

Reflections on the Touchstones

Yet, regardless of the path chosen to cross the bridge to adulthood, certain behaviors give depth to the passage and therefore carry the potential to transform the pilgrim. If young people would make the journey "heroic," they must do the following:

- search for the right path—that demands deliberation and choice;

- be willing to sacrifice for the sake of the chosen path—that gives it value;

- find someone or something to show the way—that gives direction;

- make a commitment to the task and to learning the necessary skills—that gives credibility;

- accept struggle as inevitable to the journey—that proves sufficient challenge;

- transcend the crisis—that brings insight;

- share the new understanding—that validates the transformation.

Any one of many possible paths to adulthood can be held against the above touchstones to evaluate its worth. A whole variety of experiences, no doubt, have potential gold within them if the right circumstances are in place to release it. Youth service, however, seems to possess the greatest potential to transform: to transform both our young people trying to grow up as well as our nation struggling through its own adolescence—with unresolved crises, unmet needs, undefined roles, and unfocused energy.

A Suggestion

Dave, who was with the Peace Corps in Tunisia and is now a practicing architect in business with his architect wife Libby, has a suggestion for our youth:

> I think giving them some real responsibility, some honest-to-God responsibility where they have to perform in the real world is very meaningful for kids. I think there should be an element of challenge too so that whatever is given them is slightly beyond their grasp. They really have to try for it. Then when they succeed, they learn something about what it takes to accomplish something in the real world.
>
> I don't think it should be as academic as an apprenticeship or internship. It ought to be real world, like the Peace Corps or CCC experience, where you go some place and you build something that means something to somebody. Something that has some lasting real-world value.
>
> God knows, the inner-city area of this whole country is so decayed and the infrastructure—the streets, the roads, the sewers are falling apart—kids could be trained to learn a real-world skill like finishing concrete or laying a sewer line—something physical—they would go out and actually do it in an area where the local government and the people can't afford it. The unions will fight it like hell. On the other hand, the unions could get behind it and see the potential in it as a training ground for good skilled craftsmen for the future.

The CCCs . . . if you travel around the country, many of
the finest public buildings that exist were built by the
CCC and WPA. Fine lodges and trails and murals. I've
always thought that you could teach kids some of the
traditional building and crafts skills—like iron-working,
like stone-masonry, like stone-carving—things like that
which are disappearing. If you could develop skills in
kids in those areas, they would be guaranteed
employment; they would have a skill they would be
proud of.

Our culture's most priceless resource is our kids.
This is so obvious that it's a cliché even to mention it. So, if
it is true, how can we continue to ignore, abuse, seduce and
treat them as throw-aways and problems? The good news is
that public awareness is changing. The perception of youth
as problems is shifting to that of youth as resources.[12] These
stories of young people making their heroic journeys with
courage, ingenuity, energy, and enthusiasm should spur us
elders to expand and support such opportunities for *all*
young people to earn their right to adulthood.

The mental shift out of the egocentric condition is
not easy because it calls for new ways of thinking. This is a
clue to the function of rites and rituals: They shift the focus
of attention and channel the psychological energy out of the
self into the broader community. Service, as a contemporary
rite, becomes a daily expression of the adage, "Do unto
others as you would have them do unto you." This is an
heroic invitation . . . to give the gift of self.[13]

Young people instinctively recognize they must *earn*
their adulthood. This is another clue to what rites of passage
are about—awakening young people to their identity and to
their role in life. Each young person has a gift to give. Each
has a call to the heroic journey. That urge is so urgent, that

call so compelling, that the journey *will* be made, one way or the other. We in the adult community had better listen to those calls as well and provide for our young people the healthy opportunities to make their journeys.

* * *

Epilogue

Crossing Paths

I remember the first time the young Achilles called. That was the year I was a VISTA volunteer. I was crossing a bridge at fifty-two that I had feared at twenty-two: making my own rite of passage into a new stage of life, leaving behind a career in high school teaching, and recovering from empty-nest syndrome. As a VISTA I was serving an adult literacy program in an eastern city with an acute adult literacy deficit.

The telephone rang. A male voice was on the other end: "I need help to improve my writing skills so I can contribute the way I should."

The request struck me as somewhat unusual. Typically, people want help with literacy to fulfill some kind of personal goal such as working toward a GED, getting a driver's license, or reading to their children. This caller had in mind a desire to contribute in some broader way, but his lack of writing skills was paralyzing him.

This was the young man who almost two decades before went out into the world at the age of 17 with a ninth grade education to make a life for himself. He tells me later, with pain in his voice:

> So what I did, I quit school. I look back on it now and I know there was no greater mistake than that. I don't think I've made any mistake that had the ramifications of that one. But it was done. So anyway, the children's home where I lived decided that if I wasn't going to school, they'd arrange for me to go in the Job Corps.

> I went in the Job Corps and, in a way, it was a kind of a second loss of a home. The first was being renounced by my foster parents. [He doesn't even mention being abandoned by his blood parents.] Okay, so again I have nowhere. I'm out in the world with no ties. I had no family. So what I did, I met a guy in the Job Corps and sort of tied onto him. He told me how great his family was and how I ought to come to Iowa with him. So I left the Job Corps and went out there with him.

> He lived in the city with his mother. A nice guy. I think he was like me in a way, except he had family. But I found out they weren't very parental. I think this really hurt him.

> I remember one time we were at a party . . . all of us gettin' high. You know, at the age of 17, that's what everybody was doin'. I felt so sorry for him and hurt for him so bad 'cause the drug brought somethin' really deep up in him. He put his hands in his pockets and was walking 'round the party sayin' to people, "Are you my father? Are you my father?" I felt so bad for him 'cause I knew how it was.

> Anyway I went out there with him for a while. Then I got out on my own and lived in Iowa for about two or three years. I had jobs, but I never kept a job. I'd work a job for maybe a year or so. Then I'd get frustrated and

get fired. I wanted to get a good job. I wanted to be somethin' other than a common laborer, but I didn't know how to do it. You see what I'm sayin'? I didn't have the discipline or fortitude to start creatin' ways for what I wanted by studyin' and goin' to school. Not to mention the fact that my basic skills was so poor that it was . . . I wouldn't say it was impossible, but it certainly woulda took a concentrated discipline . . . which I lacked.[1]

Achilles sighs at the realization of lost opportunities. I sigh at the tragedy of a wasted life. Poisoned by his anger, Achilles feels trapped in his own self-destructive behavior. We—our society—should know better by now, as we approach the end of the millennium, how to support the development of young lives.

What does it take to prepare a young person to face adulthood in today's world? We are reaching a new level of understanding about human development in the face of contemporary life. It's evident that in all of our communities nationwide we have a lot of remedial parenting to do. The young Achilles must find their fathers to teach them responsibility and compassion. The rest of us must shake ourselves out of our stupor. If we are to survive the growing trend toward violence then we must ensure that members of our next generation—in fact, *all* of us—find a way to "tie onto" each other and learn to work together on something bigger than ourselves.

The very survival of democracy depends on our coming together—men and women, old and young, brown, black, yellow, and white, rich and poor—to find or create institutions where our paths can cross. We need to teach each other. We need to share the mutual responsibilities for our communities. We need to "tie onto" each other. But we need to have mechanisms for that to happen.

Bonding, a timeless emotional need, has, unfortunately, become a contemporary cliché and hence great fodder for jokes. Nevertheless, we disregard its importance at our own risk. This is an essential function of rites and rituals: bonding with the community within which one is to live and work and derive the meaning of his and her lives. As the world grows smaller, bonding must expand with ever larger communities.

We met at a crossroads in our lives, the young Achilles and I, both of us looking for wisdom. This is where the paths of our journeys brought us. I was there because VISTA offered me an opportunity to serve in a way that was appropriate for my time and situation in life. But I should have had my VISTA experience, or something like it, thirty years before, when it would have awakened me from my narrow little world and prepared me earlier for active citizenship.

As beneficial as my hospital work experience was in my late adolescence, it was only a partial heroic journey. I responded to the call, but there was no separation from home. I took on a significant task, but no guardian spirit helped me to connect the world of the sick in a middle-class urban environment to larger cultural issues. I gained practical knowledge but had no working metaphor to deepen its implications. Growing up in America demands that we move beyond race, religion, and class. I didn't understand that then, but I do now.

Although I learned a number of valuable skills— observing, nursing, comforting, and communicating which I use to this day—there was no "maturity marker" to assure me that I had indeed moved into another stage of life. Graduation didn't do it for me; I simply moved on to graduate school. Unlike my friend, Achilles, who threw away his academic life too soon, I clung to mine too long. Neither of us felt that we had earned our right to adulthood.

Who knows what might have been the right opportunity for the family-starved and education-hungry young Achilles at the time of his adolescent quest for a future? Perhaps an experience with City Year or a conservation corps could have helped him grow up in a healthier way and earn his adulthood. He dropped the Job Corps in favor of the possibility of finding family in Iowa, much like the kids of the street respond to gangs in their hunger for family.

In contrast, listen to Bill reflect on his discovery of family with City Year:

> At our orientation we talked about our families and about what we wanted to get out of this experience. . . . I remember thinking how cheesy City Year could get, I mean, about the whole family and the togetherness and the blah, blah, blah. But at the end of our orientation weekend . . . we were glowing with our new family. As cheesy as it was, it was actually true!

And Bill lived and worked and learned and grew with his new family during the year that followed.

Discovering Direction

Other young Achilles have gone into the conservation corps, to City Year, to the urban corps and have found discipline and job skills and sometimes even wisdom and family in the corps, and have shaped their lives through their experiences. Their victories lay in discovering direction in their passage. Many have turned their lives around, as Bill's friend did who came to City Year from the court system. Young people learn from working with each other. Their tasks lift them out of their small worlds and bind them together for a purpose that goes beyond themselves.

From the time of the CCC, young men have contributed (literally and metaphorically) to the building of their world. They have planted trees, raised chickens, built science labs, taught English, constructed playgrounds, and tutored children. And young women, drawn to the bridges of their adolescent dreams, have responded to their calls: going to Alaska, to war-torn Europe, to Belize, to Costa Rica, to Africa, and to inner-city Washington and Boston and Dallas.

Their victories lay in trusting their calls, in overcoming their fears, in heeding their guardian spirits, in battling their beasts. And all of them—young men and young women—have been, and continue to be, victorious in making their contributions to life.

Of course, there is no guarantee that every youth corps experience will be a genuine "rite of passage." But framing an experience like a term in a youth corps with a metaphor like "the heroic journey" can help young people make sense of a significant event in their lives. Furthermore, by identifying the touchstones and supplying a vocabulary to talk about the process of growing up, we can evaluate youth service—and other coming-of-age experiences—more effectively.

Finally, and perhaps most important, young people who give their gift of service can grow up with greater assurance that they have indeed earned their *right of passage* into adulthood.

* * *

Appendix A

The Touchstones of the Heroic Journey

An Exercise in Reflection

Each of us may have made—or missed—the "heroic journey" in our own lives. Or we may be yet waiting for it to engage us. How do we know whether an effective "rite of passage" did or didn't happen to us? Or, if we feel it didn't, how do we know the appropriate touchstone to help us identify the gold along our present path? What are the experiences that provide a bridge to maturity, the passage to adulthood, the transformation of a life? Whether the life is one's own, that of one's children or students, or the young people in one's community—or even the lives of literary or cinematic figures—an exercise like this can bring insights about ways in which a series of experiences is or is not effective as a "rite of passage" and why or why not.

The touchstones provide us with a vocabulary and a "road map" for the journey. They can be especially helpful in discovering the "road blocks" and "pot holes" of life as well as giving us a means for identifying and talking about the progress of the journey.

The uses of this kind of reflective exercise are many: workshops for parents, teachers, and youth corps leaders; a format for college and youth corps orientations and retreats; a discussion outline for literature and films; spiritual reflection in religious youth groups; and personal meditation and journal work based on one's own life. Experimentation will prove its adaptability.

The Call
"Let's get a little excitement outta life!"

What was your "call to adventure"?

_____

_____

Where did your call come from?

Outside factors:

parents	school
church	community
draft board	need to make money
other_____	

Inside impulses:

need to be useful	desire to serve
desire to learn	desire for adventure
restlessness	boredom with the status quo
other_____	

What was your response?

_____

_____

_____

_____

_____

_____

_____

The Departure
"I'm outta here!"

What kind of sacrifice did you have to make for the sake of responding to the call?

_____

_____

What do you remember about the separation from home, from the comfortable, from the familiar?
Was it difficult or easy?   Explain why.

_____

_____

_____

_____

In what way did you experience a sense of independence: financially?   emotionally?

_____

_____

_____

_____

What helped you to deal with the separation and sacrifice?_____

_____

_____

_____

_____

_____

_____

249

The Guardian Spirit
"Show me where to go, what to do?"

What form did your "guardian spirit" take?
    a mentor   an orientation
    a spiritual experience   an adult friend

_____

_____

Was he/she/it effective?
Provide the guidance you needed?   Why or why not?

_____

_____

_____

_____

What kind of support system did (or do) you have in place?

_____

_____

_____

How did you become aware of your philosophy of life? How would you describe it?

_____

_____

_____

_____

_____

_____

_____

_____

Taking on the Task
"What did I get myself into?"

What was the work you took on?
    Your new role _____
    Skills you needed _____
    Qualities of character _____
    Did you have or learn them?_____
    Who or what depended on you?_____

_____

_____

Were you helped to see your work in a social context?

_____

What strikes you now about that social context?

_____

_____

_____

Did you realize, as it was happening, the impact of the experience on your development? _____
In what way?

_____

_____

_____

Did those you served identify their own needs and agree to the service? _____
If yes, how? If no, why not? _____

_____

_____

Battle with the Beast
"I can't handle it . . . help!"

What conflict or crisis did you experience?

isolation	loneliness
poverty	language
prejudice	food
health	sexual issues

What was most difficult about your situation?

_____

_____

How did you deal with it?_____

_____

_____

What help did you get?_____

_____

What did you discover about your perceived
limitations?

_____

_____

_____

_____

Did you discover a pattern to the way you deal with
difficult situations? What was it?

_____

_____

_____

_____

_____

_____

Victory
"Wow . . . I learned something!"

What did you know after your "battle" that you had not known earlier?

_____

_____

Were you aware at the time of any of the following changes in yourself:

increased self-esteem	new skills
expanded horizons	greater knowledge
increased physical strength	heightened awareness
discovery of life vocation	diminished prejudice
assurance of having earned adulthood	

Are you aware now of these changes as you look back at your experience? Explain.

_____

_____

_____

How did your perception change?

about yourself_____

_____

about your community_____

_____

about your country_____

_____

_____

Return
"I'm a new person."

How was your experience brought to closure?
      a celebration   a private acknowledgement
      a public recognition   opportunities for sharing
What was it?_____

_____

What impact did it have on you?_____

_____

What were the direct or indirect post-service benefits?

_____

_____

What effect did the experience have?
      on your relationships:
with parents _____

_____

with siblings _____

_____

with peers _____

_____

on your career development _____

_____

_____

on your life _____

_____

_____

_____

_____

In what way(s) were you transformed?

_____

_____

_____

_____

_____

Did the experience on which you are reflecting
provide an effective rite of passage for you?
 Why or why not?

_____

_____

_____

_____

_____

_____

_____

Would you recommend such an experience to
others? Explain. _____

_____

_____

_____

How could this experience have been a more
effective bridge to adulthood? _____

_____

_____

_____

_____

_____

* * *

Reflection Notes

Appendix B

Resources

The following are service organizations and service-learning resources mentioned in *Right of Passage.*

American Red Cross

Division of Youth Involvement
8111 Gatehouse Road
Falls Church, VA 22042
703/206-8363

Programs: Youth–all ages
Check phone directory for
local chapter

The Red Cross, founded in 1863 in Switzerland, is noted for service in the fields of health, disaster relief, water safety, and recreation. Local chapters have service programs to engage young people of all ages.

The Association of Episcopal Colleges

815 Second Avenue, Suite 315
New York, NY 10017-4594
212/986-0989

Summer/semester/year
College age

A consortium of twelve colleges with historic and present ties to the Episcopal Church. Provides structured opportunities for students and recent graduates of any college, any faith, to perform volunteer service in established service agencies, both domestic and international.

City Year

11 Stillings St.
Boston, MA 02210
617/927-2500

Since 1987
10 month term
Age: 17–23

City Year is the first privately financed youth corps without religious affiliation. Key features of the C.Y. experience are diversity, team-building, and multiple work assignments. Started in Boston, City Year has expanded to Chicago, Cleveland and Columbus, Ohio, San Jose, Cal., Providence, R.I., and San Antonio, Tex.

Corporation for National and Community Service

1201 New York Avenue, NW
Washington, DC 20525
800/942-2677

Since 1993
Usually a year
18 and over

Brought into existence by the 1993 National and Community Service Trust Act, the Corporation administers VISTA, AmeriCorps, and the National Civilian Community Corps (NCCC), as well as several volunteer programs for older Americans. The Corporation is committed to serving the nation's educational, environmental, human, and public safety needs. Call for specific details.

Goshen College

Division of International Education
Goshen, IN 46526
219/535-7346

Since 1968
One term
Part of academic program

Affiliated with the Mennonite Church, Goshen College introduced in 1968 a Study-Service Term, designed to send all students to a country with a culture significantly different from the U.S. The Study Service Term is a requirement for graduation.

Habitat for Humanity International

121 Habitat Street
(Collegiate Challenge – student volunteers
Americus, Georgia 31709-3498
912/924-6935

Since 1976
Since 1987)
Spring break
program

Habitat for Humanity is a non-profit, ecumenical Christian organization committed to building affordable housing worldwide. College students contribute volunteer labor through the Collegiate Challenge, an alternative spring break program coordinated by the Campus Chapters department of Habitat for Humanity.

Institute of International Education

809 United Nations Plaza
New York, NY 10017

Over 2000 programs
80 countries

Non-profit organization that administers study-abroad programs. Produces the annual IIE directory, *Academic Year Abroad.* Available at public and university libraries.

Jesuit Volunteer Corps: Northwest

P.O. Box 3928   Since 1956
Portland, OR 97208-3928   1-year commitment
503/335-8202   21 or older
Alaska, Idaho, Montana, Oregon, Washington   College degree or
                                               equivalent

Jesuit Volunteer Corps: Southwest

P.O. Box 3266   (see above)
Berkeley, CA 94703
510/653-8564
Arizona and California

Jesuit Volunteer Corps: South

P.O. Box 3126   (see above)
Houston, TX 77253-3126
713/756-5095
Alabama, Georgia, Louisiana, Mississippi, Texas

Jesuit Volunteer Corps: Midwest

P.O. Box 32692   (see above)
Detroit, MI 48032-0692
313/963-4112
Illinois, Kentucky, Michigan, Minnesota, Missouri, Ohio,
Iowa, Wisconsin

Jesuit Volunteer Corps: East

Eighteenth & Thompson Streets   (see above)
Philadelphia, PA 19121
215/232-0300
Connecticut, Maine, Maryland, Massachusetts, New Jersey, New
York, Pennsylvania, Rhode Island, Virginia, Washington, DC

Jesuit Volunteers: International

P.O. Box 25478   Since 1984
Washington, DC 20007   Two year commitment
202/687-1132   21 or older
Belize, Jamaica, Micronesia, Nepal, Peru   College degree or equiv.

Jesuit Volunteers work domestically and internationally in education
and human services while committing themselves to living a simple
life style within a community of peers dedicated to social justice and
spirituality.

The Lutheran Volunteer Corps

1226 Vermont Avenue NW
Washignton, DC 20005
202/387-3222

One year commitment
21 or older
College degree or equivalent

Lutheran Volunteers work domestically in social justice organizations while living a simple life style in a community of peers committed to social justice and spirituality.

Mennonite Central Committee

21 South 12th Street
Box 500
Akron, PA 17501
717/859-1151

Since 1920
2 yrs. domestic
3 yrs. overseas
Wide variety of skills
& levels of education

Born of hunger & need, stimulated by war, the Mennonites & Brethren in Christ carry out community development, peacemaking, and material aid, both domestically and internationally. Variety of programs for variety of ages.

National Association of Service and Conservation Corps   (NASCC)

666 Eleventh Street NW
Suite 1000
Washington, DC 20001   202/737-6272

A non-profit membership organization that provides information and technical assistance to existing and developing programs

National Service Secretariat

c/o Augsburg College, PO 200
2211 Riverside Avenue
Minneapolis, MN 55454   612/330-1299

Founded in 1966 to promote consideration of national youth service through research, publications, pilot projects, etc.

National Youth Leadership Council

1910 W County Road B
St Paul, MN 55113-1337   612/631-3672

Dedicated to developing service-oriented youth leaders at the elementary, junior, and senior level by supporting individuals and organizations that encourage youth service and leadership. *Generator: Journal of Service-Learning and Service Leadership* published twice yearly.

Opportunities 1996: Annual Volunteer Service Handbook. (First issue is 32-page magazine format.)
Berry Publishing Services, Inc.
701 Main Street
Evanston, IL 60202-9908   800/274-9447

Includes a directory of volunteer and educational opportunities as well as articles on placement, expectations, and spirituality. Rooted in Catholic volunteer tradition but transcends denominational boundaries.

The Partnership for Service-Learning
815 Second Avenue, Suite 315   Since 1982
New York, NY 10017-4594   Summer/semester/year
212/986-0989

A consortium of colleges, universities, service agencies and related organizations united to foster and develop programs linking community service and academic study.

Peace Corps
1990 K Street NW   Since 1961
Washington, DC 20526   Two year commitment
800/424-8580   College degree or equiv.

Currently serving in 93 countries in Asia and the Pacific, Africa, South and Central America, the Caribbean, Eastern Europe and the former Soviet Union. "The toughest job you'll ever love."

Points of Light Foundation
1737 H Street NW   For published information
Washington, DC 20006   on volunteerism
202/223-9186   call 800/ 272-8306

A non-profit organization that has developed a network of more than 400 local Volunteer Centers and a database (ServLink) of more than

1,500 community service programs in addition to identifying and promoting community service programs and ideas that work. *Volunteer Leadership*, quarterly magazine for leaders in volunteer mgmt. *Grapevine: Volunteerism's Newsletter*. Six issues annually.

Public Allies
1511 K Street NW, Suite 330   Since 1992
Washington, DC 20005   10 month term
202/638-3300   Age: 18-30

An opportunity for young people to apprentice with non-profit agencies and at same time gain experience in team-building, leadership skills, and conflict resolution. Programs in Washington, D.C., Chicago, Milwaukee, Raleigh-Durham, San Jose, and Wilmington, Del.

RespecTeen Youth Update
c/o Search Institute
700 South Third Street, Suite 210
Minneapolis, MN 55415   800/888-3820

Free quarterly newsletter, prepared by Search Institute, a non-profit research organization, under the auspices of Lutheran Brotherhood. Good source of statistics, stories, and resources dealing with youth.

Sojourners
Internship Director   Since 1975
2401 15th St. NW   One year commitment
Washington, DC 20009   21 or older
202/328-8842

Sojourners are committed to spiritual growth, economic sharing, serving the poor, and working for justice and peace. They live and work in Washington, D.C. Publishes *Sojourners* magazine.

Youth Service America
1101 15th Street NW, Suite 200   Since 1986
Washington, DC 20005   202/296-2992

Non-profit link for youth service programs across America. Provides developmental and technical assistance. Promotes public awareness.

* * *

Notes

Chapter 1. Rite of Passage

1. Despite the usual negative impact on young psyches, prison can become a profound rite of passage in certain instances. See, for instance, Alex Haley, *The Autobiography of Malcolm X* (New York: Ballantine Books, 1964). Also Nathan McCall, *Makes Me Wanna Holler: A Young Black Man in America* (New York: Random House, 1994).

2. See Leon Dash, *When Children Want Children: An Inside Look at the Crisis of Teenage Parenthood* (New York: Penguin Books, 1989). The genesis of the book was a six-part series of articles written for the *Washington Post* (January 26–31, 1986) based on 17 months of research in Washington, D.C.'s poorest neighborhood.

3. Joseph Campbell, in *The Power of Myth*, with Bill Moyers, Betty Sue Flowers, ed. (New York: Anchor Books, 1988), pp. 101–104, stresses the role of the elders in initiating the young. Campbell explains the dangerous situation which results when youth are left to grow up alone: "So the youngsters invent themselves, and you have these raiding gangs, and so forth—that is self-rendered initiation" (p. 103).

4. English translation by Monika B. Vizedom and Gabrielle L. Chaffee with introduction by Solon T. Kimball (Chicago: The University of Chicago Press, 1960).

5. This is in no way to condone the clitoridectomy, also called female circumcision or female genital mutilation (FGM), a brutal procedure which often causes death to the girl victims. As with any human behavior, there are aberrations, and this is a prime example. A case in Pennsylvania is testing the U.S. immigration laws regarding female asylum-seekers from Africa fleeing this custom. Described by Linda Burstyn, in "Asylum in America: Does Fear of Female Mutilation Qualify?" *Washington Post,* March 17, 1996.

6. A central message of this chapter is the often inaccurate and excessive use of the term "rite of passage."

7. This view is promoted by Professor Solon Kimball of the University of Chicago in his introduction to the English version of van Gennep's book [see note 4 above]. Van Gennep, p. xvii.

8. *Ibid.*, p. xviii.

9. David Popenoe, paraphrasing James Q. Wilson, in "The Family Conditions of America," in Henry J. Aaron, Thomas E. Mann, Timothy Taylor, eds., *Values and Public Policy* (Washington, D.C.: The Brookings Institution, 1994), p. 98.

The *New York Times* (May 28, 1995) cites another study: James Alan Fox, dean of the College of Criminal Justice, Northeastern University, in comparing 1985 to 1993, warns that the homicide rate among youth, 18 to 24, rose 65 percent, but among 14 to 17-year-olds escalated 165 percent.

A Justice Department press release (November 12, 1995) notes that "the arrest rate for weapons offenses for 18-year-old males . . . was three times higher than for males 25 to 29 and five times higher than for males 30 to 34." Based on a Bureau of Justice Statistics (BJS) Study.

10. Van Gennep (1960) describes how these stages are played out in the life-cycle rituals. See also David Cohen, ed., *The Circle of Life: Rituals from the Human Family Album*, Intro. by Gabriel Garcia Marquez, Afterword by Peter Matthiessen (San Francisco: Harper, 1991).

11. See David D. Gilmore, *Manhood in the Making: Cultural Concepts of Masculinity* (New Haven: Yale University Press, 1990).

12. See, for instance, Marla N. Powers, *Oglala Women: Myth, Ritual, and Reality* (Chicago: The University of Chicago Press, 1986), especially Chapter 4, pp. 66–78.

13. See Louise Carus Mahdi, Steven Foster, and Meredith Little, eds., *Betwixt and Between: Patterns of Masculine and Feminine Initiation* (LaSalle, Illinois: Open Court, 1987) for Victor Turner's essay, "Betwixt and Between: The Liminal Period in Rites of Passage" (pp. 3–19), as well as the series of essays dealing with transition points in human life.

William Bridges calls this stage the "neutral zone" in *Transitions: Making Sense of Life's Changes* (Reading,

Massachusetts: Addison-Wesley Publishing Company, 1980). See especially Chapter 5, pp. 111–131.

14. Erik Erikson calls this period a "moratorium." In *Young Man Luther* (New York: W.W. Norton & Company, 1958), Erikson mentions that in Martin Luther's day the monastery sometimes offered young men a moratorium, a "way of postponing the decision as to what one is and is going to be" (p. 43).

A contemporary example of temporary monkhood is a dying practice in modern-day Thailand, a country which is 95 percent Buddhist. A generation ago men would spend four months in a monastery, fasting and meditating, before taking on their roles as husbands and fathers. Today's generation spends two weeks, if that, as a temporary monk, undergoing the coming-of-age ritual. Described by Seth Mydans in "Hellbent on Progress, Thais Sidestep Priesthood," *New York Times,* March 11, 1996.

15. See Ray Raphael, *The Men From the Boys: Rites of Passage in Male America* (Lincoln: University of Nebraska Press, 1988) for his discussion of consumerism as a less than healthy aspect of coming to maturity. He makes the point that the media offer expectations but little hope of fulfillment other than consuming commodities. Consumerism invites ". . . no sacrifice, no struggle, no hazing; instead it rewards our most *childish indulgences"* (p. 18). Italics added.

16. These are symbolic experiences which are affective as much as cognitive. Victor Turner picks up a phrase of William James's—"the law of dissociation"—to show the importance of the use of masks, dances, and sounds, which dissociate young people from their familiar ways of perceiving their lives and encourage, and often force them, to think about their world and "the powers that generate and sustain them" (p. 14). Turner's essay in Mahdi.

17. William Raspberry, "The Birth of AmeriCorps," *Washington Post,* September 12, 1994.

Chapter 2. Traditional Rites

1. Hillary Rodham Clinton's book, *It Takes a Village and Other Lessons Children Teach Us* (New York: Simon & Schuster, 1996), has drawn national attention to both the proverb and the concept.

2. See, for instance, *New York Times,* "The Children of the Shadows," ten-part series, April 1993. Also Elijah Anderson, "The Code of the Streets," *The Atlantic Monthly,* May 1994, pp. 80–94.

3. Ernest T. Pascarella and Patrick T. Terezini, *How College Affects Students: Findings and Insights from Twenty Years of Research* (San Francisco: Jossey-Bass Publishers, 1991). Pascarella and Terenzini discovered, through their review of the research, that students' level of involvement and quality of effort in both curricular and extra-curricular activities are the major determinants of the impact of college on them (p. 610).

4. Some ethnic groups expect their young adults to live with parents until they marry and establish their own families.   The question critical to growing up is, Do they assume financial and home-maintenance responsibilities within their parents' household while sharing their roof?

5. See Chapter One, note 14.

6. An example of secular ritual in Asian culture is the national celebration of the emergence of young men and women into adulthood, epitomized by the Japanese Coming-of-Age Day sponsored by the government. Held every mid-January for those who will turn 20 during the coming year, it is the time when the govenment declares them adults. The ceremony is brief; officials give speeches urging the initiates to be good citizens. At the age of 20, Japanese young people gain the right to drink, smoke, and vote, but, according to some observers, many have long been smoking and drinking. The families of the young women save for years to purchase a ritual kimono, which can cost from $5,000 to $25,000. A rite which reinforces the strong sense of community to the Japanese drew a 72 percent participation in 1994. Reported by T. R. Reed, *Washington Post* correspondent at that time in Tokyo, on National Public Radio, January 9, 1995.

7. Joseph F. Kett, *Rites of Passage: Adolescence in America, 1790 to the Present* (New York: Basic Books, 1977). Kett writes that by the mid-19th century many young men left the farm for industrial and commercial jobs because of the transportation revolution (p. 145); whereas 17th century young men were usually dependent until their marriage or the death of their father (p. 30).

See also the books of Jane Addams, especially *The Spirit of Youth and the City Streets* (1909), *Twenty Years at Hull-House* (1910), and *The Second Twenty Years at Hull-House* (1930), all published by The Macmillan Company. They indicate her concern for youth coming of age in the dense immigrant neighborhoods of Chicago near the turn of the 20th century with neither good role models nor healthy leisure-time activities.

See also Michael Sherraden, "Youth Participation in America: A Historical View of Changing Institutions," *National Youth Service: An Institution for the 21st Century*, Donald J. Eberly, ed. (Washington, D.C.: National Service Secretariat, 1991), pp. 3–30.

8. See Stephen F. Hamilton, *Apprenticeship for Adulthood: Preparing Youth for the Future* (New York: The Free Press, 1992).

One example of an American variation on the apprenticeship theme takes place in New York City. Covenant House, a child-care agency that works with homeless youth and runaway young people, runs a "Rights of Passage" job-skills program for 18- to 21-year-olds. Based on a partnership with local business, it has set up training modules and supported job placement. Described by the president of Covenant House, Sister Mary Rose McGeady, in "'At Risk' Youths: How to Help" in the *Christian Science Monitor*, September 18, 1995.

9. See Donald Eberly and Michael Sherraden, eds., *The Moral Equivalent of War? A Study of Non-Military Service in Nine Nations* (New York: Greenwood Press, 1992).

10. "The Standard Coming-of-Age Party Comes of Age in Elegance and Cost," *New York Times*, March 15, 1992.

11. The age of confirmation, at least in the Catholic Church, is more flexible—and more controversial—that that of *bar* and *bat mitzvah* and may occur any time between the ages of seven and 18.

12. For an overview of religious rites of passage and additional bibliography, see Mircea Eliade, ed., *The Encyclopedia of Religion*, Vol. 12, pp. 380–403.

See also Arthur J. Magida, ed., *How to Be a Perfect Stranger: A Guide to Etiquette in Other People's Religious Ceremonies* (Woodstock, Vermont: Jewish Lights Publishing, 1996), a description of 20 different religions and their particular ceremonies, each religion with a chapter of its own. See "Initiation Ceremony" where applicable within each chapter.

13. It is interesting in this context that the boy Jesus was the age of the *bar mitzvah* when he encountered the doctors of the law in the Temple of Jerusalem. (KJV Luke 2:42-52)

14. However, the first girl in the United States to undergo the bat mitzvah was Judith Kaplan in 1922 in New York City. A sidelight: her father Rabbi Mordecai Kaplan founded the Society for

the Advancement of Judaism, the center of the Reconstructionist movement and a part of Conservative Judaism. "Jewish Controversy over Rite for Girls," *New York Times,* March 24, 1982.

15. Stephen F. Hamilton, *Apprenticeshp for Adulthood: Preparing Youth for the Future* (New York: The Free Press, 1990), p 66.

16. Ari L. Goldman, "Shopping for Sacraments" in "Religion Notes," *New York Times,* July 2, 1994.

17. The cost in the Cuban-American community of Miami can run from $8,000 to $50,000, according to Daisann McLane in "The Cuban-American Princess," *New York Times Magazine,* February 26, 1995, p. 42.

18. "Dilemma for Church: Latino Girls Coming Out," *Los Angeles Times,* February 2, 1987; "Becoming a Woman," *Washington Post,* February 6, 1994; and "Quinceanera: A Girl Grows Up," *New York Times,* February 1, 1996.

19. Bruce R. Hare, "The Rites of Passage: A Black Perspective," A Youth Development Discussion Paper (New York: National Urban League, 1982). Dr. Hare was assistant professor of sociology at State University of New York at Stony Brook at the time the report was published. He is now in the Department of African American Studies at Syracuse University. Phone conversation with Bruce Hare, February 13, 1995.

20. "Men Going to Front Lines to Reclaim Community," *Chicago Tribune,* December 12, 1990.

21. Interview with Ronnie Wooten, then Director of Progressive Life Center's Rites of Passage Program, Washington, D.C. October 18 and 27, 1994. [Budget forced cancellation in 1995.] See expanded version in Louise Carus Mahdi, Nancy Geyer Christopher, and Michael Meade, eds., *Crossroads: Quest for Contemporary Rites of Passage* (Chicago: Open Court Publishing Company, 1996).

22. "Manhood Training Opens Options in Resisting Temptation" (Religion column), *Washington Post,* April 7, 1990.

23. See Steven Barboza, *American Jihad: Islam After Malcolm X* (New York: Doubleday, 1994). Barboza distinguishes between the "greater jihad," the striving within the self, and the "lesser jihad," a permission to defend oneself when under attack (p. 18).

24. See Arnold J. Toynbee, *A Study of History,* abridged by D.C. Somervell (New York: Oxford University Press, 1947) for a

discussion of withdrawal and return of some of the major culture heroes (pp. 217–230).

25. Joseph Campbell, *The Hero With a Thousand Faces* (Princeton: Princeton University Press, 1949).

26. Arnold van Gennep, *The Rites of Passage* (Chicago: The University of Chicago Press, 1960).

27. See, for instance, Kenneth L. Woodward, "Onward, Mormon Soldiers," *Newsweek,* April 27, 1981, pp. 87–88; also Anthony DePalma, "Learning 54 Languages with a Missionary's Zeal," *New York Times*, February 10, 1993.

28. Studies showing the relationship between human behavior and religion indicate that "people who worship regularly lead healthier, more stable lives than those who do not." Cited in the *Washington Post*, February 10, 1996. Report from the Heritage Foundation: "Why Religion Matters: The Impact of Religious Practice on Social Stability."

29. Christopher Lasch, in *The Culture of Narcissism: American Life in an Age of Diminishing Expectations* (New York: Norton, 1979), describes the scene a generation ago. Robert Bellah, Richard Madsen, William M. Sullivan, Ann Swidler, and Steven M. Tipton, in their study, *Habits of the Heart: Individualism and Commitment in American Life* (New York: Harper & Row, Publishers, 1985), discovered that many of the subjects they interviewed were seeking something beyond a self-centered life, but their language put limits on ways to think about it (p. 290).

Positive signs of the search for higher values on the national level are cited in Phyllis A. Tickle, *Re-Discovering the Sacred: Spirituality in America* (New York: Crossroad, 1995). Ms. Tickle, religion editor for *Publishers Weekly*, has an ideal vantage point from which to make her observations regarding the growth and consumption of books on religion and spirituality.

30. See Charles C. Moskos, *A Call to Civic Service* (New York: The Free Press, 1988), for a brief historical overview of the influence of conscientious objection on the civic service movement (pp. 25–29).

31. Stories of the experiences from members of each of these corps are embedded in Chapters Four, Five, and Six of this book.

32. Moskos [see note 30 above] refers to public opinion polls throughout his book, especially pp. 166–169.

See also "Teenagers Attitudes toward National Service—A report on focus group discussion sessions and a survey among teenagers," for a discription of a Gallup survey in 1993. Nancy Ethiel, series ed., *Building a Consensus on National Service* (Chicago: Robert R. McCormick Tribune Foundation, 1993), pp. 32–44.

Chapter 3. Contemporary Rites

1. For an exploration of myth and symbol and their impact on psychological development, see Mircea Eliade, *The Sacred and the Profane: The Nature of Religion*, trans. from the French by Willard R. Trask (New York: Harcourt, Brace & World, Inc., 1959) and Joseph Campbell, *Myths to Live By* (New York: Bantam Books, 1972).

2. See, for instance, "Generation Depressed," *Newsweek*, July 10, 1995, p. 63.

3. Ray Raphael, in *The Men From the Boys: Rites of Passage in Male America* (Lincoln: University of Nebraska Press, 1988), discusses unhealthy aspects of consumerism. [See note 15 in Chapter One].

4. Viktor E. Frankl, *Man's Search for Meaning: An Introduction to Logotherapy*, 3rd ed., 1984 (New York: Simon & Schuster, Inc., 1959). In a final chapter added to the 3rd edition, Frankl describes a study he published in 1933 on what he called "unemployment neurosis." When people are jobless, they feel useless, he writes. This leads to a feeling of meaninglessness. The syndrome, Frankl warns, has three facets: depression, aggression, and addiction (p. 143).

5. Kenneth Keniston, in *The Uncommitted: Alienated Youth in American Society* (New York: Dell Publishing Co., Inc., 1960), emphasizes the need for courage: "the courage to be *for* something," to search for commitments and values that will give life meaning (pp. 446, 447).

6. David Elkind, in *All Grown Up and No Place to Go* (Reading, Massachusetts: Addison-Wesley Publishing Company, Inc., 1984) alerts us to the danger of "premature adulthood" caused by an erosion of traditional "markers" of maturity. Such markers that are understood by the youngsters and sanctioned by the community provide self-definition; they reduce stress on young people "by

supplying rules, limits, taboos, and prohibitions that liberate teenagers from the need to make age-inappropriate decisions and choices" (94).

7. On masculine maturity, see, for instance, Robert Bly, *Iron John: A Book About Men* (Reading, Massachusetts: Addison-Wesley Publishing Company, Inc., 1990); Robert A. Johnson, *He: Understanding Masculine Psychology*, rev. ed. (New York: Harper & Row, Publishers, 1989); Sam Keen, *Fire in the Belly: On Being a Man* (New York: Bantam Books, 1991); Michael Meade, *Men and the Water of Life: Initiation and the Tempering of Men* (Harper San Francisco, 1993); and Ray Raphael, *The Men From the Boys: Rites of Passage in Male America* (Lincoln: University of Nebraska Press, 1988).

On feminine maturity, see, for instance, Robert A. Johnson, *She: Understanding Feminine Psychology*, rev. ed. (New York: Harper & Row, Publishers, 1989); Dr. Laura Schlessinger, *How Could You Do That?! The Abdication of Character, Courage, and Conscience* (New York: Harper Collins Publishers, 1996), and Gloria Steinem, *Revolution From Within: A Book of Self-Esteem* (Boston: Little, Brown and Company, 1992).

On dependency of adult children, see Susan Littwin, *The Postponed Generation: Why American Youth Are Gowing Up Later* (New York: William Morrow and Company, Inc., 1986); Cheryl Merser, *"Grown Ups": A Generation in Search of Adulthood* (New York: G.P. Putnam's Sons, 1987); Jean Davies Okimoto and Phyllis Jackson Stegall, *Boomerang Kids: How to Live with Adult Children Who Return Home* (Boston: Little, Brown and Company, 1987); Dr. Larry V. Stockman and Cynthia S. Graves, *Grown-Up Children Who Won't Grow Up: How to Finally Cut the Cord That Binds You* (Rocklin, CA: Prima Publishing, 1994) .

8. *The Postponed Generation*; *"Grown-Ups";* and *Boomerang Kids.* The latter book suggests guidelines for coming home as well as criteria for readiness to separate again. *Grown-Up Children* offers a "Parents' Bill of Rights."

9. *The Forgotten Half: Pathways to Success for America's Youth and Young Families.* Youth and America's Future: The William T. Grant Foundation Commission on Work, Family and Citizenship, November 1988.

10. See Elijah Anderson, "The Code of the Streets," *The Atlantic Monthly, (*May 1994), pp. 80–94. Also Bruce R. Hare "Black Youth at Risk," *The State of Black America 1988* (New York:

National Urban League, Inc., 1988), pp. 81–93; Kay S. Hymowitz, "The Teen Mommy Track," *City Journal* (Autumn 1994), pp. 19–29; Malcolm Klein, *The American Street Gang: Its Nature, Prevalence, and Control* (New York: Oxford University Press, 1995), and Luis J. Rodriguez, *Always Running: La Vida Loca: Gang Days in L.A.* (New York: A Touchstone Book, 1993).

11. During the editing stage of *Right of Passage*, Daniel Goleman published *Emotional Intelligence* (New York: Bantam Books, 1995). Goleman, based on his research on dealing with anger and depression, uses the term "reframing" as a way of reinterpreting one's circumstances more positively (pp. 60, 74).

12. The Phillips Collection, Washington, D.C., December 12, 1992 – April 4, 1993.

13. See also Erving Goffman, *Frame Analysis: An Essay on the Organization of Experience* (New York: Harper & Row, 1974).

14. Werner Jaeger, *Paideia: The Ideals of Greek Culture*, 2nd ed., trans. Gilbert Highet (New York: Oxford University Press, 1945), especially Chapter 2, "The Culture and Education of the Homeric Nobility," pp. 15–34.

15. Don McAdams, Northwestern University psychology dept., in *The Stories We Live By: Personal Myths and the Making of the Self* (New York: William Morrow and Company, Inc., 1993), states that we create our myths or stories in order to give meaning to our lives. "The stories we live by are made, not found," he writes (p. 274). James Fowler, "Stages of Faith," *Psychology Today* (November 1983), uses the term "master story" to describe what one's life is all about (pp. 56–62). This "master story" may be conscious or unconscious.

Robert Bellah *et al*, in *Habits of the Heart* (New York: Harper & Row, 1985), point to an important role of "communities of memory": retelling their stories, providing examples of "men and women who have embodied and exemplified the meaning of the community" (p. 153).

16. The film *Hoop Dreams* and the book *The Last Shot* by Darcy Frey (Houghton Mifflin, 1994), for instance, depict young men who seek their redemption through basketball. The dream of basketball glory rules their lives from their teen years into their early twenties.

17. Eric Berne in *What Do You Say After You Say Hello?: The Psychology of Human Destiny* (New York: Grove Press, 1972), defines "script" as "an ongoing program, developed in early childhood under

parental influence, which directs the individual's behavior in the most important aspects of his life" (p. 418).

See also Joseph Campbell, *Myths to Live By* (New York: Bantam Books, 1972) and Rollo May, *The Cry for Myth* (New York: W.W. Norton & Company, 1991) for a discussion of the role of myths in framing one's reality. For a reference to myths from a sociological perspective, as "important sources of meaning," see Bellah, *Habits of the Heart,* p. 40.

18. See Jolande Jacobi, *The Psychology of C. G. Jung* (New Haven: Yale University Press, 1973).

19. Both books—*Postponed Generation* and *Grown-ups*—point to the importance of concern about the world beyond one's personal boundaries, but neither suggests specific ways to develop this awareness. *Postponed* features several interviews with young people who have a religious structure in their lives. In contrast, other interviewees who are drifting through life give the impression their alienation comes from lack of structure and purpose. This may be a hint that religious affiliation helps ward off alienation by connecting one to the broader community, but this idea is not developed in either book.

20. The National Foundation for Teaching Entrepreneurship has come up with an interesting idea. In addition to teaching high school students the practical skills of setting up and running a business, program instructors are using stories of the struggles of contemporary entrepreneurs to teach lessons in persistence, courage, and adherence to a dream.

21. Recent publications, both magazines and books, point to hunger for spirituality. The *New York Times* best-seller list has included several books addressing spiritual issues for the past year, in some cases longer. Phyllis A. Tickle, religion editor for *Publishers Weekly*, documents the rise in spiritual interest in her book, *Re-Discovering the Sacred: Spirituality in America* (New York: The Crossroad Publishing Co., 1995).

22. Pascarella and Terezini, in *How College Affects Students,* (pp. 17–47) give a helpful overview of psychological theories of maturation. [See Chapter 2, note 3.]

23. Anne Frank, *The Diary of a Young Girl* (New York: Pocket Books, 1958) and Nathan McCall, *Makes Me Wanna Holler: A Young Black Man in America* (New York: Random House, 1994).

24. Abraham Maslow, *Motivation and Personality* (New York: Harper & Row, 1954) and *Towards a Psychology of Being* (New York: Van Nostrand, 1962).

Viktor E. Frankl, in *Man's Search for Meaning: An Introduction to Logotherapy*, [see note 4] describes his experience in a concentration camp. Because his basic needs had been satisfied earlier in his life, he was able to withstand enormous deprivation in the camp and move into a high level of psychological and spiritual development. While Maslow's theory suggests that higher development would have been impossible unless the lower needs had been satisfied adequately earlier in life, it does not guarantee that the latter will ensure the former.

25. Urie Bronfenbrenner, in *The Ecology of Human Development: Experiments by Nature and Design* (Cambridge: Harvard University Press, 1979) emphasizes the importance of role-shift in the maturing process.

Another striking example of the impact of new roles on juvenile development is a program in Bellflower, California. Delinquent teenagers, mostly males, are matched one-on-one with disabled students. They work together two hours each day. The average time span together is about six months. One of the at-risk youngsters speaks for all when he says, "I never had anyone need me before." *Washington Post*, November 7, 1990. Telephone interviews, June 1994, with the lead teachers, Cedric Anderson and Sandy Osborn, and the designer of the program, Sharon Roberts.

26. See Erik Erikson, *Childhood and Society* (New York: Norton, 1963) for his developmental chart identifying the seven stages of life and their respective challenges.

27. Mihaly Csikszentmihalyi and Reed Larson, in their study of adolescence from the perspective of teenagers' internal feelings, discuss the importance of restructuring psychic energy (p. 14). *Being Adolescent: Conflict and Growth in the Teenage Years* (New York: Basic Books, Inc., Publishers, 1984).

28. See William James, *The Principles of Psychology*, Vol. I (New York: Dover Publications, Inc., 1890), especially Chapter Four, for his classic observations on habit: "The great thing, then, in all education, is to make our nervous system our ally instead of our enemy" (p. 122).

"Habits of the heart"—a term coined by Alexis de Tocqueville —is used by Bellah and his colleagues [see note 15] to describe the mores of a society, that is, traditions and practices which can give us important insights into a culture. Alexis de Tocqueville, *Democracy in America,* George Lawrence, trans., J.P. Mayer, ed. (New York: Doubleday: Anchor Books, 1969), p. 287. Cited in Bellah, p. vii.

29. A year-long study by researchers from four universities verifies pervasive "psychologically harmful" televised violence and points out the risks of excessive viewing: imitation, desensitization, and fear of attack. Cited in the *Washington Post,* February 6, 1996.

30. "Not Like the Movie: 3 Take a Dare, and Lose," *New York Times,* October 19, 1993; also "'Program' Scene Cut After Teens Hit by Cars," *Washington Post,* October 20, 1993.

31. See David I. Macleod, *Building Character in the American Boy: The Boy Scouts, YMCA and Their Forerunners, 1870–1920* (Madison: The University of Wisconsin Press, 1983) for an early history of the Boy Scouts, originally an institution for building character in middle class boys. More recently The Greater New York Council created Scoutreach in 1989 to set up scouting programs for inner-city youngsters. "Blazing a Trail in the Inner City," *New York Times,* January 9, 1994.

32. For a history of Outward Bound, see Joshua L. Miner and Joe Boldt, *Outward Bound U.S.A.: Learning Through Experience in Adventure-Based Education* (New York: William Morrow and Company, 1981).

33. Many men, especially the World War II generation, considered their military service a rite of passage, a journey to adulthood.

34. See the reflective exercise in Appendix A as an aid to thinking about a personal rite of passage.

35. Louise J. Kaplan, Ph.D., *Adolescence: The Farewell to Childhood* (New York: Simon and Schuster, 1984), p. 240.

36. See Dorothy Stoneman with John Bell, *Leadership Development: A Handbook from the Youth Action Program of The East Harlem Block Schools* (New York: Youth Action Program, 1988).

37. See Cecilia I. Delve, Suzanne D. Mintz, Greig M. Stewart, eds., *Community Service as Values Education* (San Francisco: Jossey-Bass Inc., Publishers, 1990) for the rationale and strategies for incorporating reflection into service programs.

See also materials from the National Youth Leadership Council for the use of reflection with service programs for lower, middle, and high school. Address in Appendix B.

38. "Confirmation" in the interpersonal sense was first used by Martin Buber. "Distance and Relation," in *The Knowledge of Man,* ed. Maurice Friedman, trans. Maurice Friedman and R.G. Smith (New York: Harper & Row, 1965), p. 71. Buber shows the importance of acknowledgement and recognition by significant others to the development of human relationships.

39. Viktor E. Frankl, *Man's Search for Meaning.* Frankl's description of "unemployment neurosis" is in the final chapter (pp. 139–154), added to the 3rd ed. and based on his lecture at the Third World Congress of Logotherapy, Regensburg University, West Germany, June 1983. Regrettably, there is no indication of a follow-up study. The social chaos of the time no doubt precluded it. [See also notes 4 and 24 of this chapter.]

Diane Tice, a psychologist at Case Western Reserve University, in her research on strategies people use to escape foul moods, discovered that engagement in volunteer work is a powerful mood-changer. Cited in Daniel Goleman, *Emotional Intelligence* (New York: Bantam Books, 1995), p. 75.

40. Frankl, p. 142.

41. One example is the court judgment that Leona Helmsley's employees may have done some of her community service, a portion of her penalty for tax evasion. "Extra Community Service, U.S. Tells Leona Helmsley," *New York Times,* September 16, 1995.

42. Volunteer work, now the expectation for the Miss America candidates, is supposed to be as sexy as their swimsuits, their formal wear, and their talent performance. "Here She Is, Miss America, Whose Ideal?" *New York Times,* September 16, 1995.

Part II. The Heroic Journey

1. Joseph Campbell, *The Hero With a Thousand Faces,* 2nd ed. (Princeton: Princeton University Press, 1968).
2. William D. Dinges, "Joseph Campbell and the Contemporary American Spiritual Milieu," in Lawrence Madden, ed., *The Joseph Campbell Phenomenon: Implications for the Contemporary Church* (Washington, D.C.: The Pastoral Press, 1992), pp. 9–40,

places Campbell in historical context and points to some critical problems with the monomyth theory. In spite of reservations about Campbell's theory, I have seized the metaphor of the "heroic journey" because it offers a stimulating and helpful way to think about the coming-of-age process.

3. The vocabulary I have borrowed from Campbell includes "the call," "departure," and "the return." I was also inspired by participating in Paul Rebillot's "Hero's Journey" workshop in Chicago in 1976. See Paul Rebillot, with Melissa Kay, *The Call to Adventure: Bringing the Hero's Journey to Daily Life* (San Francisco: Harper, 1993). Rebillot developed the "Hero's Journey" as a kind of ritual-drama process for giving a group of participants access to their inner imaginative journey. While I believe that this process can be helpful, I have discovered through my own experience and research that life itself can provide scenarios that invite us to maturity if we have the skills and a workable metaphor (such as the heroic journey touchstones) to frame our experiences for reflection.

4. David D. Gilmore, *Manhood in the Making: Cultural Concepts of Masculinity* (New Haven: Yale University Press, 1990), p. 226.

Chapter 4. It's Hard to Let Go

1. William James, "The Moral Equivalent of War," *International Conciliation*, no. 27, 1910. Later published in *Essays on Faith and Morals* (New York: Longman, Greens, 1943), pp., 311–328.

2. See Stephen F. Hamilton and L. Mickey Fenzel, "The Impact of Volunteer Experience on Adolescent Social Development: Evidence of Program Effects," *Journal of Adolescent Research*, Vol. 3, No. 1, Summer 1988, pp., 65–80.

See also Donald Eberly and Michael Sherraden, eds., *The Moral Equivalent of War? A Study of Non-Military Service in Nine Nations* (New York: Greenwood Press, 1990) and Donald Eberly, ed., *National Youth Service: A Global Perspective* (Washington, D.C.: National Service Secretariat, 1992).

3. See Jean Houston, *The Hero and the Goddess: The Odyssey as Mystery and Initiation* (New York: Ballantine Books, 1992), Chapter 11, "The Initiation of Telemachus," pp., 267–299.

4. Mihaly Csikszentmihalyi and Reed Larson, *Being Adolescent: Conflict and Growth in the Teenage Years* (New York: Basic Books, Inc., Publishers, 1984), pp., 71–74.

5. See Marc Freedman, *The Kindness of Strangers: Adult Mentors, Urban Youth and the New Voluntarism* (San Francisco: Jossey-Bass Publishers, 1993). Provides good advice for mentoring programs.

Chapter 5. This Wasn't What I Bargained for

1. See Karen Schwarz, *What You Can Do for Your Country: An Oral History of the Peace Corps* (New York: William Morrow and Company, Inc., 1991) for additional examples.

2. It was Stephen R. Covey who alerted me to the necessity of moving beyond independence in growing up. To be truly mature demands interdependence. *The 7 Habits of Highly Effective People* (New York: Simon and Schuster, 1989). This is also a theme woven through *Habits of the Heart* by Bellah *et al.*

3. The recognition and appreciation of the interdependence of all life and the wise use of resources as characteristics of adulthood, I suggest, is another way of saying that maturity is the capacity for love and work, first noted by Sigmund Freud.

4. See Suzanne Goldsmith, *A City Year: On the Streets and in the Neighborhoods with Twelve Young Community Service Volunteers* (New York: The New Press, 1993), Chapter 1, pp. 5–15, for a description of the composition of the teams.

5. William Bridges drew my attention to the importance of "disenchantment" on the path to maturity. He makes an important distinction between disenchantment and disillusionment; the first is necessary, the second regressive. *Transitions: Making Sense of Life's Changes* (Reading, Massachusetts: Addison-Wesley Publishing Company, 1980), pp. 98–102.

Chapter 6. Something Happened

1. Ray Raphael in *The Men From the Boys: Rites of Passage in Male America* (Lincoln: University of Nebraska Press, 1988) tells the

story of a high school graduate who took on a personal challenge of a hike in the Rocky Mountains (p. 66). It was a difficult hike, but no one was there to give value to his experience, no one to tell him he had changed. He later reflected that he wanted to remember this as a significant experience. Yet everything felt the same as before.

2. Raphael, *ibid.*, comments that the ultimate initiation is to come close to death but survive, perhaps the ultimate achievement of manhood (p. 34). But for Vietnam veterans, the community at large did not offer a meaningful incorporation back into the body politic.

Robert Bly, in *Iron John: A Book About Men* (Reading Massachusetts: Addison-Wesley Publishing Company, Inc., 1990), comments that the suicide rate of Vietnam men is higher than the death rate during the war (p. 197). Mr. Bly doesn't indicate, however, the source of this information.

3. Fred Hargadon, Address to High School Parents, The North Shore Country Day School, April 19, 1988. Follow-up interview, Princeton University, April 30, 1991, with the author.

Part III. Right of Passage

1. Tom Singman, "Navel Maneuvers," *New York Times Magazine* (January 22, 1994), p. 20.

2. See Leon Dash, *When Children Want Children: An Inside Look at the Crisis of Teenage Parenthood* (New York: Penguin Books, 1989); Bruce R. Hare, "Black Youth at Risk," *The State of Black America 1988* (New York: The National Urban League, 1988), pp. 81–93; and Kay S. Hymowitz, "The Teen Mommy Track," *City Journal* (Autumn 1994), pp. 19–29, for a discussion of life-scripts which lead to teenage pregnancy.

3. Developed by an education research team from Boston University and tested in Wellesley Middle School in Wellesley, Mass. Described in the *Christian Science Monitor*, February 14, 1995.

4. One example is the National Institute for Responsible Fatherhood and Family Development, a private program on the east side of Cleveland founded by Charles Ballard. 8555 Hough Avenue, Dept. P, Cleveland, Ohio 44106.

5. Such research fed into a model program developed by the Emory University/Grady Hospital Teen Services in use throughout the state of Georgia. Called the "Postponing Sexual Involvement"

program, it was conceived in 1985. Making use of an educational strategy called "social inoculation," the program trains high school students to give presentations to middle school youngsters not only on the social influences to engage in sex but the skills to think about and deal with the pressures. An unanticipated outcome is the benefit to the student leaders: a boost in self-esteem that comes from recognition and respect from their younger students. Marion Howard and Judith Blamey McCabe, "Helping Teenagers Postpone Sexual Involvement," *Family Planning Perspectives*, Vol. 22, No. 1 (January/February 1990), pp. 21–26.

Chapter 7. The Journey Beckons—Paths

1. The National and Community Service Trust Act of 1993.

2. One example is the Center for Interim Programs, P.O. Box 2347, Cambirdge, Mass. 02138. Phone: 617/547-0980. Cornelius Bull, who founded the Center 15 years ago, goes so far as to say, ". . . no one should go to college [directly] out of high school." Interview in the *Christian Science Monitor*, August 28, 1995.

3. See Urie Bronfenbrenner, *The Ecology of Human Development: Experiments by Nature and Design* (Cambridge: Harvard University Press, 1979). Bronfenbrenner's emphasis on the importance of role change on the development of the young personality is particularly relevant in looking at service experience as a rite of passage. New roles bring new expectations and evoke new behavior.

4. See Appendix B for names and addresses of programs.

5. See Suzanne Goldsmith, *A City Year: On the Streets and in the Neighborhoods with Twelve Young Community Service Volunteers* (New York: The New Press, 1993).

6. See Gail Sheehy, *Spirit of Survival* (New York: William Morrow & Company, 1986). Also Emmy Werner and Ruth Smith, *Overcoming the Odds: High Risk Children* (Ithaca: Cornell University Press, 1992). Werner's book includes a point that is especially significant in thinking about service as essential to adolescent development: "At some point in their young lives usually in mid-childhood and adolescence, the youngsters who grew into resilient adults were required to carry out some socially desirable task to prevent others in their family, neighborhood, or community from

experiencing distress or discomfort" (p. 205). Quoted from S. Rachman, "The Concept of Required Helpfulness," *Behavior Research and Therapy*, 17, pp. 1–6.

7. See Marc Freedman, *The Kindness of Strangers: Adult Mentors, Urban Youth, and the New Voluntarism* (San Francisco: Jossey-Bass Publishers, 1993).

8. See Mihaly Csikszentmihalyi and Reed Larson, *Being Adolescent: Conflict and Growth in the Teenage Years* (New York: Basic Books, Inc., Publishers, 1984) and Marc Freedman, *Kindness*.

9. See Erik Erikson on "generativity," a key challenge to people in middle-adulthood and older. "Identity and the Life Cycle," *Psychological Issues* (Vol. 1, No. 1, 1959). Erikson developed a chart showing the life stages and their respective challenges. [See Chapter 3, note 26.]

10. *AmeriCorps*VISTA 30th Anniversary Newsletter* (January 1995).

11. Anthony DePalma, "Learning 54 Languages with a Missionary's Zeal," *New York Times*, February 10, 1993.

12. See Donald Eberly and Michael Sherraden, eds., *"The Moral Equivalent of War? A Study of Non-Military Service in Nine Nations*, Forward by Amitai Etzioni (New York, Greenwood Press, 1990), especially Chapter 2, pp. 7–18, "Canada: Katimavik and Cultural Integration."

Chapter 8. The Journey Beckons—Opportunities

1. See Michael Sherraden, "Youth Participation in America," in Donald J. Eberly, ed., *National Youth Service: A Democratic Institution for the 21st Century* (Washington, D.C.: National Service Secretariat, 1991), pp. 3–30, for a historical view of the labor market and the educational system and why they are currently inadequate institutions for bringing young people to adulthood.

2. Suggested by Eberly, *National Youth Service*, pp. 38–39.

3. *Ibid.*, p. 35.

4. The Corporation for National and Community Service now serves this purpose.

5. In fact, it is a national bargain. See Nancy Ethiel, series ed., *Building a Consensus on National Service*, The Cantigny Conference

Series (Chicago: Robert R. McCormick Tribune Foundation, 1993), p. 14.

6. The Ford Foundation study: Richard Danzig and Peter Szanton, *National Service: What Would It Mean?* (Lexington, Mass.: Lexington Books, 1986). Cited in Steven Waldman, *The Bill: How Legislation Really Becomes Law: A Case Study of the National Service Bill*, revised and updated (New York: Penguin Books, 1995), p. 21.

7. Information from the director of the Jesuit Volunteers International, October, 1995.

8. Information from the director of the Lutheran Volunteer Corps, October, 1995.

9. See Eberly, *National Youth Service,* pp. 40–42, for a discussion of allocation of funds. See also Charles C. Moskos, *A Call to Civic Service: National Service for Country and Community* (New York: The Free Press, 1988), pp. 155–160, for a discussion of the funding of a national service program.

10. At the time I was developing my own ideas about "moving from me to we," Amitai Etzioni published his book, *The Spirit of Community: Rights, Responsibilities, and the Communitarian Agenda* (New York: Crown Publishers, Inc., 1993), in which he points to a deficit of "we-ness" in our society (p. 26). He further recommends that we move from "I" to "we" (pp. 25, 26).

William F. Buckley, Jr., in *Gratitude: Reflections on What we Owe to our Country* (New York: Random House, 1990), makes a compelling argument for universal voluntary national service. He reminds us that " . . . what severs the cords binding the generations also snaps the web that unites contemporaries" (p. 15).

11. By Bok for the *Akron Beacon Journal,* March 5, 1993.

12. I was reminded of the medieval French parable when I saw it again in the *Generator: Journal of Service-Learning and Service Leadership* (Winter 1996), p. 16. [*Generator* is published by the National Youth Leadership Council. See Appendix B.]

13. Joseph O'Donoghue and Mary Ann O'Donoghue researched and authored the report, "The Peace Corps Experience: Its Lifetime Impact on United States Volunteers." Cited by Carol Kleiman in "Join Peace Corps and Be a Success," *Chicago Tribune,* January 24, 1988. For college graduates of 1996, the Peace Corps emerges as "the employer with the most job openings" according to

the *Washington Post*, March 22, 1996. The plan is to recruit 3,292 new graduates.

14. Copies are available through the program directors of faith-based volunteer corps, such as the Jesuit, Lutheran, and Mennonite Volunteer Corps.

Chapter 9. Getting There

1. The first type of work-study experience, the College Work-Study Program (CWSP), was initiated under Title IV of the Higher Education Act of 1965. The second type is the Cooperative Education Plan, originally developed by Northeastern University in Boston.

2. Donald J. Eberly, in *National Service: A Promise to Keep* (Rochester, N.Y.: John Alden Books, 1988), describes the intent and the weaknesses of CWSP. See especially pp. 209–211.

3. Allen Wutzdorff, "The What, Why, How, and Where of Interning," *The National Service Guide* (New York: Access, n/d), p. 55. Wutzdorff is the executive director of the National Society for Experiential Education. [*The National Service Guide* is no longer available.]

4. See *The National Directory of Internships* (Raleigh, N.C.: National Society for Experiential Education). Contact 3509 Haworth Drive, Suite 207, Raleigh, NC 27609-7229, or call 919/787-3263 for the latest edition.

Also see Nella Barkley, *How to Help Your Child Land the Right Job (without being a pain in the neck)* (New York: Workman Publishing, 1993) for a variety of ideas on moving from the world of school to the world of work. Especially valuable for its Resource section, pp. 300–343.

5. A good brief historical overview of apprenticeship can be found in Stephen F. Hamilton. *Apprenticeship for Adulthood: Preparing Youth for the Future* (New York: The Free Press, 1990), pp. 63–67.

6. Hamilton's book as a whole is a compelling argument for learning from the German system to construct an American system of apprenticeship.

7. Hamilton, p. 169.

8. "Job-Training Program Is Seen as U.S. Model," *New York Times,* December 27, 1993. "More Schools Mix ABC's with Tooling for a Trade," the *Christian Science Monitor,* February 10, 1994.

9. Public Allies. See Appendix B for address and phone.

10. See Stuart W. Showalter, ed., *The Role of Service-Learning in International Education: Proceedings of a Wingspread Conference* (Goshen, Indiana: Goshen College, 1989) for ways in which service-learning is leavening higher education. Shows the range of possibilities in college-level service-learning at universities such as Stanford and Michigan State as well as at the Episcopal colleges and Goshen, the pioneers in the process.

11. See Robert Coles, *The Call of Service: A Witness to Idealism* (New York: Houghton Mifflin Company, 1993) for ideas about relating service experience to literature and reflection.

12. Bonnie Bernard, "Youth Service: From Youth as Problems to Youth as Resources," *Prevention Forum* (January 1990), pp. 6–10. See also Donald J. Eberly, ed., *National Youth Service: A Global Perspective* (Washington, D.C.: National Service Secretariat, 1992), p. 33, where youth are described as "an opportunity, not a problem."

One example of the renewed perspective of youth as resources is the AFL-CIO plan to hire 1,000 young interns during the summer of 1996 to work in unionization drives. The model is Freedom Summer of the '60s, the civil rights movement. "Labor Uses an Old Idea to Recruit the Young," *New York Times*, February 25, 1996. I predict that the infusion of youthful energy and enthusiasm will transform the long lethargic labor movement.

13. Ernest Becker, in *The Denial of Death*, says, "If you are going to be a hero then you must give a gift" (p. 173). Quoted in McAdams, p. 226.

Epilogue: Crossing Paths

1. As *Right of Passage* goes to press, Achilles is making his own rite of passage through the Twelve Steps of Narcotics Anonymous (N.A.). The process bears an uncanny resemblance to the "heroic journey," another confirmation that the journey must be made one way or another. Surely our nation's communities can offer other options before people's lives reach this point.

* * *

Index

285

Index

Initiation,
    Catholic rituals 29–38
    contemporary 17–18
    spiritual 52–53
    tribal 12–17
Interdependence 15, 128–129
Internships 228–229
Islam
    adult responsibility 39–40
    coming of age 38–40
    community 39
    identity 40
    jihad 43, 268n.23
    Nation of 42–43
    parents 25, 38
    practices 25, 40
    reading *Qur'an* as rite of passage
        39

Jail,
    McCall's experience 63–65
    as rite of passage 43
James, William
    on habit 274n.28
    law of dissociation 266n.16
    moral equivalent of war 82
Jesuit
    International Volunteers (JIV) 86,
        110, 127–128
    modeled on work camps 53
    service corps support 209–210
    Volunteer Corps (JVC) 90–91,
        95–97, 103–104,133–134,
        144–146, 162–164
Job Corps 231
Judaism
    bar/bat mitzvah 25–28
    in Canada 29
    Israel, trip to 28–29
    parents 25, 28, 29
    practices 25
    service, concept of 28
Jungian psychologists 61

Law in religious communities 50
Life crises
    challenge of adulthood 62–65
    focus of rite of passage 13
    inevitability of 56
Lutheran
    confirmation 33–34
    parents 33–34
    responsibilities 34
    service, concept of 34

Lutheran Volunteer Corps (LVC)
    experience 105, 123, 130–131
        159–160, 161–162
    modeled on work camps 53
    service corps support 210

Malcolm X 43
Maslow, Abraham
    hierarchy of needs 65–66
    relevance to rites of passage 66
Mass media 7-20
    cultural expectations 68
    description of teens 17, 88
Maturity
    benchmarks of 56–58
    characteristics of 129
    dealing with crisis 62–65
    destination of 79
    emotional 59
    focused energy 68
    framing life 59–62
    heroic sacrifice 78
    markers of 50, 56–58, 270n.6
    materialistic criteria 58, 59
    new roles 67–68
    satisfying needs 65–66
    social 65
McCall, Nathan 63–65, 67
Mennonite
    Goshen College program 86, 233
    as peace church 53
    service, role of 208–209
    volunteer corps experience 85–86,
        97, 137–139, 173–174
Mentoring
    African American 41–42
    awareness of 112
    in internships 228
    origin of "mentor" 102
    personal 107–112
    role of elders 101–102
    in service corps 186–189
    by site supervisors 138, 228, 230
    Telemachus 102
Metaphor
    bride of Christ as 34
    definition 5
    heroic journey as 43–44, 177
    hero's journey as 44, 77–78
    as myth 61–62
    rite of passage as 7–20
    as script 61–62
Military
    call of the warrior 82–83
    experience 83, 84, 119, 133, 170

About the Author

Nancy Geyer Christopher, mother of three, earned her Ph.D. in interdepartmental studies (theater, religion, and anthropology) at Northwestern University. She taught anthropology and psychology for a dozen years in the upper school of The North Shore Country Day School in Winnetka, Illinois. During that time she analyzed the school as an example of enlightened progressive education, just one generation removed from John Dewey. The combination of analysis and stories of the people who created the school in 1919 (especially the founding headmaster Perry Dunlap Smith) and those who nurtured that vision are preserved in her first book, *The North Shore Country Day School: Seventy Years of a Community of Learning* (1993).

Her background in anthropology, her close contact with high school students, and her years of exploring the original vision of the School, convinced her that some kind of "rite of passage" experience is not merely a nice thing to do, but is in fact a developmental necessity. It can take many forms, but one of the most effective, given the nature of American democratic society, is an intensive service experience in a youth corps. Recognizing that she had missed a part of her own growing up process, she became a VISTA volunteer at the age of 52 with the Literacy Volunteers of America in Washington, D.C., to discover what that might bring to her experience as an adult citizen.

Currently, Nancy Christopher and her husband, a former journalist and national association executive, conduct workshops and speak nationally on the subject of this and her other books.